CW00585131

BERNEY ARMS REMEMBERED

Sheila Hutchinson

Sheila Hutchinson

Front Cover Photograph: The Berney Arms High Mill, 1953, before it was repaired by the Ministry of Works. Note there is no fantail on the mill. Photograph kindly supplied by Keith Rackham.

Back Cover Photograph: Henry Hewitt, known as 'Yoiton' lived at Ashtree farm, Berney Arms, and was the last marshman to work the Berney Arms windmill. He is seen here at the Norfolk Show sometime in the 1950's. Note he is wearing Buskins. Photograph supplied by Carol Goreham.

Berney Arms Remembered

ISBN 0-9541683-2-1

Published
By
Sheila & Paul Hutchinson
7, Colman Avenue,
Stoke Holy Cross,
Norwich,
Norfolk.
NR14 8NA
e-mail address:-
sheila@hutchson.freeserve.co.uk

Printed
By
RPD Litho Printers
Gorleston
Norfolk

CONTENTS

Berney Arms Remembered

Acknowledgements:

It has been a great pleasure to meet up with many people who have lived, worked, and played on and around the Berney Arms marshes, having been warmly welcomed into many of their homes for a good old yarn about how it once was. I wish to thank them all.

I wish to express many thanks to the following people and organizations for their help in providing valuable information and permission to reproduce photographs, information and tales for this book; without their help this book would not have been possible.

Mr Peter Allard. Mr Gerald Banham. Mr Andrew Barton. Mr Mike Browne. Mr Peter Browne. Mr Charlie Carter. The late Mr Jack Carter. Mr Ron Carter. Mrs Janet Church (nee High). Mr Mike Davison. Mr Trevor Dyble. Mr Dick Flowers. Mrs Thelma French. Mr Sid Gibbs. Mr & Mrs Trevor and Carol Goreham (nee Brackenbury). The late Mrs Dorothy Hanton (nee Carter). Mr & Mrs Derek and Gillian Havis. Mr & Mrs Stanley and Barbara Hewitt. Mr Micky Hewitt. Mr Ernest Hewitt. Mrs Millie High (nee Hewitt). Mr & Mrs Sonny and Myra Horton. Mr William James. Mrs Teresa Leech (nee Hewitt). Mrs Susan Loughlin. Mr Bob Mace and the late Mrs Violet Mace (nee Hewitt). Mr Ivan Mace. Mr Robert Malster. The late Mr Reginald Mathews. Mrs Elsie Matthews. Ms. Marguerite Matthews. Mr Vincent Pargeter. Mr Mike Pickard. Mr David Pyett. Mr Keith Rackham. Mr Edward Roberts. Mr Jim Rowe. Mr David Schwartz. Mrs Linda Smith (nee Hewitt). Mr Arthur C Smith. Mr Anthony J. Ward. Mr Ray Walpole. Mr Sid Ward. Mr Derek Williams. Mr John Willimott. Eastern Daily Press, Eastern Evening News, Great Yarmouth Mercury, Norwich Record Office. Great Yarmouth and Norwich Libraries.

Special thanks go to Paul Hutchinson for all his encouragement, help with research, preparation of sketch plans and maps, scanning of photographs, and the typing of the book for publication.

Every effort has been made to establish copyright for the photographs used in this book but in some cases this has proved impossible. Anyone with a copyright claim is asked to contact the publisher in writing.

Disclaimer:

Much of the information herein is from people's memories and therefore it may contain some errors as often people's memories are less accurate than they believe, and often people contradict each other. I have tried to check the accuracy but I apologise for any errors that may be present, and I cannot accept responsibility for the consequences of any errors and omissions.

Information from census returns may also be inaccurate for several reasons, for example: handwriting is often not clear and sometimes impossible to read, the information supplied may not always be the full truth, many people were illiterate and could not write or spell their names, and in early censuses the exact age was not required.

DEDICATION.

I dedicate this book to my daughter Karen Ann Black, her husband James Hunter Black,
my grandson James Callum Black and my granddaughter Keira Marie Black,
and to all our children to let them know how their ancestors once lived.

INTRODUCTION

After publication of the 'Berney Arms: Past and Present' I had many people getting in touch with me, some with tales to tell and others with many old photographs. The 'Berney Arms: Past and Present' book has now sold out and I am still being asked for it. Rather than do a reprint of that book I have done this new one with many different old photographs, which show more about life at Berney Arms as it once was.

After seeing the Berney Arms Past and Present book many people, past residents and their relations and friends, wanted a reunion at the Berney Arms Inn. The first reunion took place two years ago and over 80 people attended. A third reunion is planned for September of this year (2003).

Berney Arms was a small hamlet in the parish of Reedham and takes it's name from the Berney family who owned these marshes. This book, however, covers the area from Seven-Mile House up to Lockgate Farm and I have included sketches of the Tithe maps. As before I have included the census information but updated with the 1901 census and extra information.

Much of the factual information was in the previous book. History will always be the same, unless new information is found.

Berney Arms Remembered
RAILWAY AND BERNEY ARMS STATION

The Yarmouth and Norwich Railway was given approval in Parliament on 18th. June 1842. The first phase of the railway to be built was the Yarmouth to Reedham section, upon which work was commenced in April 1843 and employed about 1500 men. It cost about £200,000. Samuel Morton Peto was in charge of the railway construction and the main contractor was George Merritt. The engineers were Robert Stephenson (chief) and G.P. Bidder. The single-track line was officially opened on 1st. May 1844.

All the materials for the railroad construction, along with the locomotives and carriages, were brought into Great Yarmouth by sea.

Being built across the flat marshland this section of line is fairly straight and no difficult tunnelling or engineering was required, however precautions were necessary when laying the tracks to prevent them from sinking into the marshland. Before laying the tracks a bed of faggots was sunk into the ground and then piling with ballast was carried out to give a firm foundation for the tracks.

A station or 'halt' was provided at Berney Arms as a result of an agreement of 6th June 1843 between the Yarmouth and Norwich Railway and Thomas Trench Berney, the landowner. Berney agreed to sell the land providing the railway company would maintain a station there in perpetuity. The Yarmouth and Norwich Railway also laid an electric telegraph in 1844, making this the first line in the country to have block signalling.

In 1845 the Yarmouth and Norwich line became part of the Norfolk Railway.

The first ever Yarmouth to Norwich Railway timetable dated 3 May 1844 did not mention Berney Arms, however, in a timetable alteration issued by the Norfolk Railway on 1st November 1846 we have shown two Down trains from Norwich to Yarmouth calling at Berney Arms at 10:37 and 21:22, and two Up trains at 10:06 and 19:06 on weekdays. There were also two trains each way on Sundays.

In 1850, as a result of a lack of passengers using the Berney Arms Halt, the railway company decided to no longer halt their trains at Berney Arms and argued that the original agreement in 1843 specified a station but omitted to specify that the trains should stop. A legal confrontation ensued and continued until 1860 when the company agreed to stop one train each way on Mondays, Wednesdays, and Saturdays, and T.T. Berney was also given £200 compensation. The railway company anticipated the outcome of the legal battle and services were in fact recommenced in 1855.

In January of 1852 George Merritt was awarded the permanent way maintenance contract for the Yarmouth to Norwich line.

Berney Arms Halt is the smallest station in Britain with only one platform. The platform was originally about sixty paces long but it is now only about twenty-four paces. The west part, the part now in use, has been built-up with wooden sleepers and has a cinder surface.

In the 1950's when steam trains had several carriages the train would pull up with the guards van at the platform and the locals would always use the carriage near the guards van. Any goods for delivery to, or collection from, Berney Arms, such as milk churns, the mail, water churns, groceries etc. were always placed in the guards van.

By the 1970's the population at Berney Arms was very low with only the pub and Ashtree farm being occupied, yet the 1983/84 timetable showed 7 Up trains to

Figure 1. Top: Down train with a Steam Engine No 62611, D16/3 4-4-0, entering Berney Arms Station, circa 1954 (A. Barton). Left: Members of the Yachting club waiting for a train at Berney Arms circa 1953, (K. Rackham). Right: Diesel train leaving Berney Arms for Gt. Yarmouth in 1960.

Figure 2. Albert Hewitt, railway ganger living at the Station cottages and working at Berney Arms in 1953 (V. Mace).

Norwich each weekday and 4 Down trains to Yarmouth, with 5 trains in each direction on Sundays

Today's trains usually have only two carriages and are Anglia Railways Class 150 type, and the passengers have to contact the guard as soon as they get onto the train to request him to stop the train at Berney. He opens the door for them. To request a train to stop while standing on the platform it is necessary to put your arm out like you would when requesting a bus to stop. Not all trains passing through Berney Arms, however, will stop when requested and the Wherry Lines timetable for 2000/01 shows only one Up request train per day at 14:25 and two Down request trains at 08:02 and 11:00 on weekdays. Sundays are much better with four request trains in each direction. The trains on this route have been Paytrains since 1967 with tickets issued by the guard.

Figure 3. Henry Hewitt 'Yoiton' putting his milk churns onto the train going to Reedham in 1960.

There was no proper lighting on the platform until 1952 when the locals complained that it was dangerous and the railway gave in and erected some lights. The then station mistress Violet Mace, or her father Albert Hewitt who also worked for the railway, would light them and refill the containers with paraffin, which would be delivered by the guard.

In 2002 a bicycle rack was provided on the station platform for the locals but no bike has yet been seen here, and on 7th May 2003 a small wooden shelter was erected at the back of the platform. It has side windows and holes in the back so that the wind does not blow the roof off and will allow people to watch the birds.

SIGNAL BOX

There was a wooden signal box, which when we lived at Berney Arms, was worked only in the summer months. It operated four signals, home and distant for each direction. In the winter months all four signals were left in the raised position and the signal box was unmanned.

Although this was a single line, Berney Arms signal box was an intermediate block post, which divided the Reedham to Breydon section during times of peak summer traffic. Berney Arms had no passing loop so the only benefit was with closely following trains, which was the way the summer traffic operated. The Great Eastern Railway used the Tyer Permissive Tablet instrument between Reedham Junction and Breydon Junction without involving Berney Arms, but Tyer's one-wire, three-position block instruments were provided at Reedham, Berney Arms and Breydon Junction.

This was probably not the first signal box at Berney Arms. When Violet Mace and her father Albert Hewitt moved to the station cottages in 1947 there was an old disused wooden signal box at the side of their back garden. It had inside a copper for boiling clothes and was used as a wash-house. This old box was slightly smaller than the signal box that was in use.

Figure 4. The cycle rack on the Berney Arms platform

Figure 5. Berney Arms Station Cottages in 1969 (P. Allard)

During the 1950's and early 1960's there was a bell on the west station house wall outside the living room window. It was worked from the Reedham signal box to warn that the train was on its way. Dorothy Hanton recalled that there was a brief period when the bell did not work. When someone from the railway company came to investigate the problem they discovered that someone had jammed an old sock into it to stop the noise.

One of the men to work the signal box was a Mr Hammond who lived at Yarmouth, and he would get the last train back to Yarmouth. The signal-box, which was in use until the early 1960's was bought by Mr Manning and moved to the pub in 1964 where he used it as a storeroom. It is still at the back of the pub. Kavan Hunt, who lived in the station cottages, had the switchgear box and kept his ferrets in it.

In the 1950's there was also a black shed standing near the signal box. It was built of sleepers and was tarred black, and was used by the railway workers as a store for their equipment.

There was also a GPO red telephone kiosk situated near the station marsh gate in the 1950's. This too was bought by Mr Manning and moved to the pub.

Figure 6. Violet Mace, Berney Arms postmistress and station mistress, taking a telephone message at the station / post office in 1953 (V. Mace).

STATION HOUSES. (TG460053)

The station buildings were built at the same time as the railway in the 1840's and were built of red brick and slate, and were semi-detached cottages. One of the rooms in one of the cottages was used as the Post Office, rail ticket office and waiting room and there would be a blazing coalfire in the winter. Like most of the other houses in Berney they had no electricity, nor running water, and had a brick cistern and barrels to catch the rainwater from the roof. In later years the Hunt family had churns of water delivered from Yarmouth by train.

During the 1953 floods, although the railway line was not badly damaged at Berney the station cottages were flooded. Eliza Hewitt living here at the time of the floods died shortly afterwards.

When Bob and Violet Mace were at the station cottages during the 1950's their rent was 8s 9d, and they could have bought the pair of cottages for £50, but refused the offer, and later in 1956 moved to the Island. When the Hunt family lived in the adjacent station cottage in the 1960's they too had the opportunity to buy the cottages, for £250, but also declined and moved away in 1969. Shortly afterwards the station cottages were demolished.

Mr Tibbenham, a local builder, and Stanley Hewitt pulled down the station houses. Tibbenham took away some of the roof slates and Stanley used the bricks for filling the ruts on the marsh tracks and much of the wood. Stanley used his tractor to help knock down the building. The footings for the station buildings are still visible today but are overgrown and fenced off.

Figure 7. Joseph Williams, nicknamed Paddy, from number 1 cottage, being served at the post office by Violet Mace in 1953 (V. Mace).

Berney Arms Remembered

POSTAL DELIVERIES.

The mail was delivered to, and collected from, the Station by train and the Berney Arms post office was incorporated into the station house.

Several of the Berney locals took on the job of delivering the post to the residents of the eleven dwellings at Berney Arms and to some of the people living in the nearby marsh houses by the Halvergate Fleet. Some of the local resident who took on the delivery round were:-

Fred Hewitt, 1930's; Violet Hewitt (later Mace), 1938/9; Millie Hewitt (later High), early 1940's; Dennis Appleton, 1940's; Elsie Bailey, late 1940; Reginald Matthews, early 1950's; Mr Archie Hitchcock, late 1950's; Dorothy Hanton, temporary relief in 1950's for Violet: Henry Hewitt 'Yoiton', circa 1960.

Seven Mile House had their post delivered by the Reedham postman/woman.
Lockgate Farm and marsh house had their post left in a box next to the railway line.

Figure 8. Postman Arthur Best arriving from Gt. Yarmouth at Berney Arms Station to deliver the mail circa 1980, photograph by Les Gould courtesy of EDP (Archant).

After the Berney Arms station cottages were pulled down there was only a few remaining Berney residents and the postal deliveries were then made from Yarmouth and a postman was sent down by train three times a week. By 1980 the deliveries were down to once a week, according to an article in the Yarmouth Mercury on 18th January 1980.

Mr Arthur Best (of Yarmouth), 1970 to 1980, ref. G.Y. Mercury 18:01:1980 and Mr Dick Salmon, ref. Daily Mirror 1970 were two of the three Yarmouth postmen.

Today no post is delivered to Berney and the few residents have to collect their mail.

Berney Arms Remembered

Some Occupants and Staff at Railway Cottages:

Name	Description / Notes.
Thomas Johnson	Stationmaster / Postmaster 1908
Fred Greengrass	Stationmaster / Postmaster 1916
Mr Bertie Staff	Signalman circa 1928
Thomas & Eliza Hewitt family	circa. 1891 to 1910. (East house). He was a blacksmith and worked for the railway as a platelayer / ganger.
Mr & Mrs Runacles	circa.1920's till 1947. (West house). She was Post & Station mistress, Mr Runacles was signalman & railway ganger. He died on Christmas Eve, 1946, after collapsing on the platform.
Albert Hewitt & daughter Violet	From 1947. (West house). He was Railway Ganger & She was Station & Postmistress.
Bob and Violet Mace, with their son Brian & Violet's father Albert	Violet Hewitt married Bob Mace and she remained as Station & Postmistress till 1956 when they all moved to the Island.
Eliza Hewitt	1940's till 1953. (East house). Retired widow. Her granddaughter Patricia lived here with her for a time.
Unoccupied	The East cottage was unoccupied for a couple of years after Eliza died and was used on Saturdays for the local Reedham clergyman to give a 'Sunday School' for local children.
Rose & Dick Howard	From 1956 (West house) She was postmistress & he worked for railway.
Ralph & Elvera Hunt & family	Circa 1957 till 1969. (East house). Ralph worked for railway.

SEVEN-MILE REEDHAM

This area, which is about seven miles along the river Yare from Great Yarmouth, is an interesting area, which has been the home of three windmills, two steam pumps, a diesel pump and an electric pump, all of which were used for draining the marshes. There were also two dwellings here, Seven-Mile House next to the river and another cottage near to Polkey's mill. Only a short distance away a row of three railway cottages was also erected in the 1840's when the Norwich to Yarmouth railway line was built. These railway cottages were located in the parish of Wickhampton

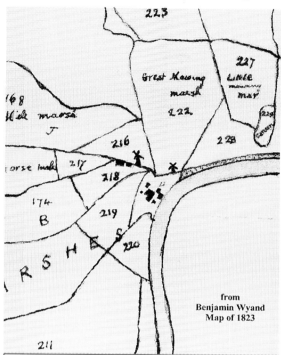

from Benjamin Wyand Map of 1823

Figure 9. The area around Seven-Mile, Reedham from the 1823 map. Polkey's and Cadge's mills are shown but the North Mill is absent. The buildings by the river are Seven-Mile House and the buildings in plot 218 are where the Thaxter family lived.

From the Reedham Tithe Apportionment we have the following: Joseph Thaxter is listed as occupier of areas numbered 80, 81 and 92, 93, 94, and John Francis Leathes is listed as the owner of these lands. The mill known as 'Polkey's Mill', and a marsh house stand on plot 80, which is listed as 'Cottage, Mill & Garden'. It is reasonable to assume that the Thaxter family lived here and worked Polkey's Mill.

Areas 82 to 84 are also owned by John Francis Leathes and are occupied by Mary Jary. Area 82 is listed as 'Mill and Yard' and is the site where the 'North Mill' is located. John Francis Leathes was the Lord of the Manor of Reedham and the major landowner.

Robert Burgess is listed as occupier of areas 76 to 79 and 99 to 111 and the owner is listed as Rev. William John Emmitt. Seven-mile house stands on plot 104, listed as 'House & garden', while Cadge's Mill is situated at the junction of plots 77,'Garden & Marsh', 78, 'Rand' & 79, 'Mill Marsh'. Although the map shows a circle with a dot inside, similar to the markings for the other mills, the inventory, does not actually list a mill here, even though a mill was at this location on Bryant's earlier map and on the later O.S. maps. Perhaps the mill was not functional at this point in time.

Berney Arms Remembered

It is reasonable to assume that the Burgess family lived at Seven-Mile house and, operated Cadges Mill, when it was there.

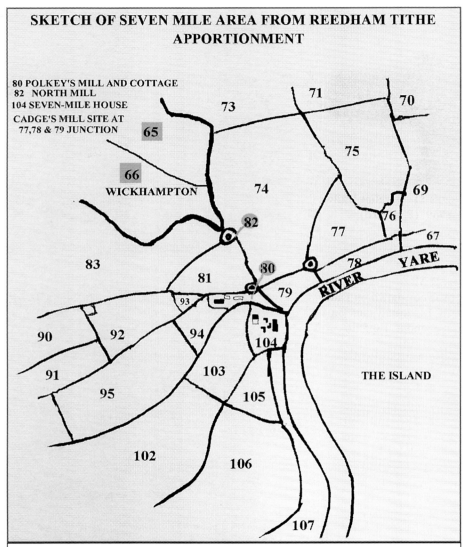

SKETCH OF SEVEN MILE AREA FROM REEDHAM TITHE APPORTIONMENT

80 POLKEY'S MILL AND COTTAGE
82 NORTH MILL
104 SEVEN-MILE HOUSE
CADGE'S MILL SITE AT
   77,78 & 79 JUNCTION

WICKHAMPTON

THE ISLAND

RIVER YARE

Figure 10. A sketch of the Seven-Mile Area, produced from the Reedham, and Wickhampton, Tithe Apportionment Maps, circa 1841. Area 66 in Wickhampton was owned and occupied by James Miller while area 65 was owned and occupied by Amy Rudd. These two areas were known as Hulver Coat Marshes. The Railway cottages were built in area 65 in the mid-1840's.

Figure 16. Riverboard workers piling the river wall where it had been breached earlier by the 1953 floods. Seven-Mile House is seen in the background on the left. The man on the left is Alan Brackenbury. (C. Goreham)

Figure 17. Sketch of Polkey's Mill in 1959 by Mike Browne.

Berney Arms Remembered
POLKEY'S MILL (TG445035)

This mill was marked on Faden's map of 1797 and on all subsequent maps. It has also been known as 'Seven Mile Mill' and 'South Mill' and the current name is thought to be after a marshman 'Polkey' Thaxter who worked the mill for many years. The present mill was probably built between 1840 and 1880. It drove a scoopwheel and on the floodgate it has inscribed 'Barnes'. This probably refers to Richard Barnes, a millwright of Southtown, Great Yarmouth who was active in the 1860's through to the early 1880's.

It was a black, tarred brick tower mill of medium height, which had patent sails, an eight-bladed fantail and a boat-shaped cap. The mill last worked in about 1941. Ivan Mace remembers a chef from a pub had the mill in the early 1960's but he didn't like the coypus and left the area. Most of the machinery remains inside the mill. A temporary aluminium cap, fitted in about 1980, and the remains of the sails were still attached until recently when restoration work began. The sails were removed 26th March 2003.

Polkey's mill – update 16/3/03 by Vincent Pargeter

Polkey's Mill is the first Broads drainage mill to be restored under the "Land of the Windmills" project.

The work at Polkey's Mill started in Spring 2002 when a crushed concrete causeway was constructed to create an access to the mill for vehicles from the concrete road to Seven Mile House. Later in the year, the decayed floors were removed from the mill and taken away for repair. A close inspection of the floor beams revealed that they had formerly been floor beams in a wooden octagonal "smock" type windmill, and that the joists had been braces and studs in the wall framing of such a mill. Some of the joists were pieces cut from former canvas-rigged windmill sails, one with a cleat still attached. These sails had rotated clockwise rather than anti-clockwise, an unusual feature still present in Polkey's mill today.

The Polkey's smock mill timbers were jointed in the same way as those found in Dutch smock mills, and differ from English practice. The Fenland smock mills were framed in this way, and they were the direct descendants of the mills built or designed by the Dutch when they were called in to advise on Fenland drainage in the 16th and 17th centuries. Thus the Polkey's timbers are of considerable historic interest, and may be quite old. It should be pointed out that Herringfleet Mill smock mill, built 1830, has English-style framing. One can deduce that a former smock mill on or near the Polkey's site was demolished, and some of its components used in the construction of the present brick-built mill.

As work has progressed at Polkey's, it has become obvious that the mill has been altered considerably during its life. The tower has been raised at least once, and possibly twice. The cap is designed to be turned by a tailpole like High's Mill Halvergate, and has been converted to fantail winding at a later date. The head wheel and wallower were once almost equal in size, and were wooden "trundle gears" like those in High's Mill. They are now cast-iron gears of nineteenth century date, installed to step-up the gear ratio so that the patent-shuttered sails could revolve more slowly than the previous cloth-covered ones.

Figure 18. Top left: Polkey's Mill in 1899 (Allard), right: Cadge's Mill in 1930's (Allard), Bottom: Cadge's Mill in February 2002 (Hutchinson).

Berney Arms Remembered

It seems that Polkeys Mill was considerably modernised in Victorian times, increasing its power and water-lifting capacity. This, together with the steam pump, was probably what made the North Mill redundant. A cast-iron bedplate for the outer scoop wheel bearing carries the inscription "England Millwright Yarmouth"

In 2003, work has continued on Polkey's Mill, and the floors have now been rebuilt, retaining a fair proportion of the original material. The scoop wheel and its shaft have been taken out for repair, and the cap and sails will shortly be removed for the same reason. It is proposed to carry out the repairs to the tower, cap and machinery in 2003, and fit the new sails in Spring 2004.

CADGE'S MILL (TG446036)

Figure 19. Reggie Hewitt working on the sails of Cadge's Mill circa 1941. (L. Smith)

This was known as Cadge's or Kedge's Mill, but the origin of the name is not known. It has also been called 'Batchies Mill' and 'Stimpsons Mill'. It was marked on Faden's, Wyand's and Bryant's map as a drainage mill, though not named, but it is not clear from the Tithe Apportionment if a mill was here around 1840. The land where the mill stands, was owned by the Rev William John Emmitt at the time of the Tithe Apportionment.

The current mill was probably built about 1880. It has been suggested that when it was first built it had buckets attached to the scoopwheel, but that this was not very successful. The scoopwheel was inside the mill. This was a 4 storey high tarred brick tower mill with two doors, patent sails, an 8 bladed fantail and a typical boat shaped cap.

The scoopwheel was sixteen feet in diameter and the paddles 14 inches wide. It was last worked in about 1941 and Ivan Mace recalls that the sails of this mill were later removed and taken away to be put onto another mill elsewhere. This mill had a fireplace inside, probably not so much for keeping the operator warm but more for preventing the internal water lane from freezing up in severe weather.

The controls, switchgear and transformer for the new electric pump were installed in this mill in the early 1980's, and a flat corrugated roof was fitted.

Under the 'Land of the Windmills' project Cadge's mill is to be given a new cap and new sails, and to be fitted with a full set of shutters and the full winding gear. The mill suffers from damp and the water lanes into the mill are to be

Figure 20. Cadge's Mill June 1974. (A.C. Smith)

opened up and fitted with grills. The millwright Richard Seago was appointed to do the restoration work, but the work may actually be done by Vincent Pargeter.

In recent months it has been suggested that the mill could be not only restored but that a generator could be located inside the mill so that it could generate electricity.

STEAM PUMP (TG446035)

This was built in about 1880, and has the inscription 'J.W.R. 1880'. This refers to John William Rose of Reedham Hall, who was listed as Lord of the Manor of Reedham in the 1883 directory and who owned many of the marshes near to Thaxter's marsh house and Polkey's mill. It may have been built to replace an earlier steam drainage mill at TG447036, or simply as an aid for the adjacent Polkey's mill. It was last worked in about 1941 when the diesel plant took over.

The building is constructed of brick, with cast iron window frames and the roof is corrugated iron sheeting. The interior walls of the building were covered in pine panelling and the floors were black and white tiles.

The engine was a single cylinder horizontal engine with a 12-inch bore and 24 inch stroke. It was fitted with Meyer expansion gear and produced about 75 horsepower. This drove a turbine pump through 'double bevel gears' and a countershaft. The engine was built by Richard Barnes, a millwright of Great Yarmouth. The lift of water from dyke to river was about 5 to 7 feet.

The pump was probably operated by either the Thaxter family or the Burgess family who lived in the adjacent marsh houses. A Mr Bob Burgess is believed to have been one of the last men to operate the steam pump.

Ivan Mace recalls that there was a deep well next to the steam pump where the water was always cool. Jack Farrow who lived at the Seven-mile railway cottages used to get his drinking water from this well. He made a yoke frame to strap across his shoulders so he could carry two buckets of water at a time across the marshes.

Much of the machinery of the old mill was sold in the 1960's as scrap metal.

The tall chimneystack blew down in 1976 during the winter gales, but most of the buildings of this old steam mill are still in existence.

Under the 'Land of the Windmills' project driven by the Norfolk Windmills Trust and the Broads Authority, and funded by the Broadland District Council, a Heritage Lottery grant and a grant from WREN (Waste recycling environmental body), this engine house is due for repair. It has been suggested that it could become a 'museum' building open to visitors arriving by boat, and that new river moorings will be made next to Seven Mile house.

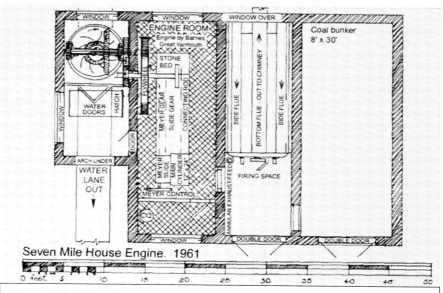

Figure 21. Floor Plan of the Steam Pump Engine House at TG446035 drawn by A.J. Ward.

STEAM PUMP (TG447036)

Possibly this was a predecessor of the above steam mill and lay to the east of the diesel plant. It was not marked on any of the early maps (ie Faden's, Wyand's, Bryant's or the

Figure 22. Top: Steam Pump House and Polkey's Mill in 2002, Bottom: Ruins of the earlier Steam Pump House in 2002. (Hutchinson)

Reedham Tithe map) and so was probably built around 1850. It was probably last used in the 1880's. A few brick remains are visible showing sluice bay and housing for a scoop-wheel. A.J. Ward has suggested that the scoop-wheel may have been 3 feet wide and about 20 feet in diameter. No photographs of the old pump house have been found and it is not known who built it. The land where it was built was, at the time of the Tithe Apportionment, circa 1840, owned by the Rev William John Emmitt.

DIESEL PUMP (TG447036)

This was built in 1941 and had 3 single cylinder Ruston and Hornsby engines supplied new in 1941 by William Foster & Co. Lincolnshire. It has a concrete floor and 3 foot walls

Figure 23. Diesel Pump House at Seven-Mile in 2000. (Hutchinson)

supporting steel framing clad with corrugated sheet metal, painted green. Two engines power the centrifugal pumps marked Gwynnes, and the other, a starting engine with 2 flywheels, drives a Ruston and Hornsby air compressor and a suction priming pump. Outside is a cistern holding cooling water and a tank for holding diesel fuel. Fuel was delivered by boat. It was last used in the early 1980's and was superseded by an electric pump. After the 1953 floods Reggie Mace had this pump working continuously for 3 days. It is now in the care of The Norfolk Windmills Trust and is still functional, and could be used in an emergency. The alterations to the river wall currently being done mean that this pump may need to be moved if it is to be preserved.

TUCKS MILL. (TG461044)

This was a drainage mill and though not marked on Faden's Map of 1797 it did appear on Wyand's Map of 1823, suggesting it was built sometime in the early 1800's. On Bryant's Map of 1826, it was labelled as 'Berney's Mill', suggesting it was owned by the Berney estate.

On the Reedham Tithe Apportionment map, circa 1840, it is marked in area 53 as 'Mill, Yards and Rand' and was owned by the Reedham Lord of the Manor John Francis Leathes and 'occupied' by a Thomas Sibel. Leathes owned some of the other nearby marshes, numbered 48, 49, 50 and 57, but the adjacent marshes to the west and north of the mill were owned by the Rev John Emmitt and a Mr John Green. Thomas Sibel was also listed as the 'occupier' of area 52 and 56 but he was not found listed in the 1841 Reedham census.

The mill was also shown on Ordnance Survey Maps of 1835-37, 1884, 1904, 1913 and 1926 where it was shown as a drainage windpump.

It is possible that it may have been rebuilt at some stage in the late nineteenth century and may not be the original mill, which was built sometime before 1823.

The last mill was a brick tower mill of average height and tarred. It carried four patent sails, which turned anti-clockwise into the wind. These were double shuttered with 9 bays, with 3 shutters in each bay and a total of 54 shutters per sail. The mill had a boat-shaped cap with no gallery and carried an 8-bladed fantail. The sails were adjusted with a chain guide pole with a Y-wheel. It drove a large scoop wheel, but no details of size are available.

Within living memory, this mill has always been known as Tuck's Mill. It is possible that the name may have come from a landowner, since in the 1864 White's directory there is a Rev. G.D. Tuck listed as a major landowner in Reedham and in the 1883 directory another major landowner is listed as C.E. Tuck. It is possible that the Mill was rebuilt for one of these Tucks, hence the name.

The surrounding marshes and the mill became the property of Arthur Stimpson in the early part of the twentieth century.

Tuck's mill was the responsibility of Mr Fred Burgess of Seven Mile House in the 1930's, and he employed Jack Farrow, who lived at No.1 Cottage, Berney Arms near the 'strip' to operate the drainage mill.

On 26th April 1941 the sails were caught by the wind from behind and because the brake had not been fully applied they began to turn backwards. The friction started a fire destroying the cap and the sails. The burning sails looked like a Catherine wheel. The mill was not hit by a bomb, but bombs were dropped on the strip once the mill was alight. Jack Farrow was an elderly man with bad legs and was unable the put out the fire.

The brick shell stood for several years until about 1950 when Reginald Matthews who owned the Berney Inn at the time bought the shell for £100 from Stimpson. He employed someone to dismantle the tower brick by brick, and used the bricks to build a septic tank at the inn and make other repairs to the inn. Reg Mathews came to Berney Arms from Sussex and recalls that the 32 foot long wooden upright shaft from the mill 'disappeared' one weekend when he went back to Sussex for a few days.

Figure 24. Tuck's Mill in working order (P. Allard). The cottages 1 to 4 are seen on the right and Ashtree farmhouse on the left.

The area where this mill once stood is now owned by the RSPB.

The footings of Tuck's Mill were uncovered in 1999 but they are now overgrown once more.

The alterations to the river wall being carried out at the present time, which will move the wall back many metres, could place the foundations on the rond.

Figure 25. Top. A wherry sailing past Tuck's Mill, date unknown (Allard).
Bottom. Tuck's Mill is shown on the left and the two buildings on the right
are the remains of the brickworks buildings which were located at
TG462044 between Tuck's Mill and 1 to 4 cottages. The people shown are
raising 'The Lowestoft Trader' in May 1910. (Hobrough)

Berney Arms Remembered
INFORMATION FROM THE REEDHAM TITHE APPORTIONMENT.

Note: Various dates are given on the documents from 28th Dec 1839, including 5th Jun 1840, & 28th Sept 1841.

Thomas Trench Berney was listed as the main landowner at Berney Arms owning the areas numbered 1 to 47 inclusive on the Tithe Map and he owned some 363Acres.

The Berney Inn stands on the plot, number 27, and was then 'occupied' by a Mr William George. William George does not appear in the 1841 Reedham Census and the Inn was probably actually inhabited by someone else in the employ of Mr George.

There was a Brick-ground shown on plot 30 which had 2 squares marked on it. These squares may be hard-standing areas or buildings associated with the brickworks. It was listed as owned and occupied by Thomas Trench Berney.

The cement works was listed as 'Factory, Mill and Yards' and was on plot 32. It was listed as owned and occupied by Thomas Trench Berney. The Berney Mill and the bungalow were not marked as separate buildings but would be part of these factory buildings.

James Duffield was listed as 'occupier' of areas 1 to 21, 31, and 33 to 47, and the owner was again Thomas Trench Berney. Ashtree Farm is on plot 34, the Cottages known as 6&7 are on plot 31, with Cottages 1 to 4 on plot 38.

Plot 37 has 2 squares marked on it but is simply called 'Marsh'. This area, plot 37, was shown on the earlier Wyand's map as a brick-ground and the squares must have been buildings associated with the brickworks.

It is probable that James Duffield, who appears in the 1841 and 1851 censuses as a marsh farmer, lived in the big house, Ashtree Farmhouse, but who lived in the cottages is impossible to say. They may have been occupied by the families who worked for James Duffield, or perhaps were uninhabited at that time.

Other landowners owning neighbouring marshes were:

John Francis Leathes, the Lord of the Manor of Reedham at that time, who owned areas 48, 49, 50, 57, known as Leathes' Marsh and which were 'occupied' by a Robert Browne, and plot 53 the site of Tuck's mill, 'occupied' by Thomas Sibel.

John Green who owned and 'occupied' areas 54, 55, 59 and 60.

Philip Blundell Nesbitt who owned marshes 61 to 65, known as 'Monks Marshes' and which were 'occupied' by George Nislen.

Rev John Emmitt who owned areas 51, 'occupied' by a Samuel Warnes, and 52 and 56, which were 'occupied' by Thomas Sibel.

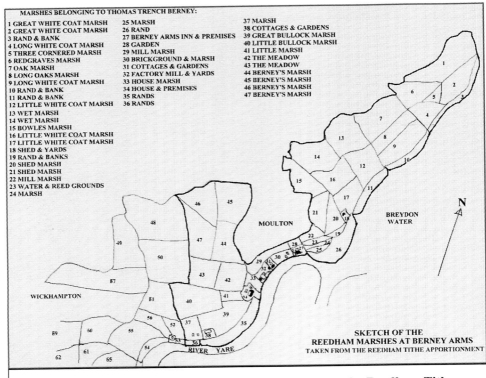

MARSHES BELONGING TO THOMAS TRENCH BERNEY:

1 GREAT WHITE COAT MARSH
2 GREAT WHITE COAT MARSH
3 RAND & BANK
4 LONG WHITE COAT MARSH
5 THREE CORNERED MARSH
6 REDGRAVES MARSH
7 OAK MARSH
8 LONG OAKS MARSH
9 LONG WHITE COAT MARSH
10 RAND & BANK
11 RAND & BANK
12 LITTLE WHITE COAT MARSH
13 WET MARSH
14 WET MARSH
15 BOWLES MARSH
16 LITTLE WHITE COAT MARSH
17 LITTLE WHITE COAT MARSH
18 SHED & YARDS
19 RAND & BANKS
20 SHED MARSH
21 SHED MARSH
22 MILL MARSH
23 WATER & REED GROUNDS
24 MARSH
25 MARSH
26 RAND
27 BERNEY ARMS INN & PREMISES
28 GARDEN
29 MILL MARSH
30 BRICKGROUND & MARSH
31 COTTAGES & GARDENS
32 FACTORY MILL & YARDS
33 HOUSE MARSH
34 HOUSE & PREMISES
35 RANDS
36 RANDS
37 MARSH
38 COTTAGES & GARDENS
39 GREAT BULLOCK MARSH
40 LITTLE BULLOCK MARSH
41 LITTLE MARSH
42 THE MEADOW
43 THE MEADOW
44 BERNEY'S MARSH
45 BERNEY'S MARSH
46 BERNEY'S MARSH
47 BERNEY'S MARSH

MOULTON
BREYDON WATER
WICKHAMPTON
RIVER YARE
N

SKETCH OF THE
REEDHAM MARSHES AT BERNEY ARMS
TAKEN FROM THE REEDHAM TITHE APPORTIONMENT

Figure 26. Map of the Berney Arms Area taken from the Reedham Tithe.

BRICKWORKS (TG462044)

A brickworks once existed on the marsh next to 1-4 Cottages and was shown on Wyand's Map of 1823 as 'brick grounds'; on Bryant's map of 1826 as 'kilns'; on the Ordnance Survey Map of 1835 as 'Brickyard', and as 'Old Brick Yard' on the 1890 OS map. The tithe map, circa 1840, however, list this area only as 'Marsh', suggesting that the brickworks or brick grounds at this location were no longer in use. The Tithe Map indicates two buildings at this location and the two buildings were still shown on the 1913 O.S. map. These buildings may have been the old brick kilns mentioned on Bryant's map.

COTTAGES 1 TO 4 (TG462044)

These cottages were shown on Wyand's map of 1823 and were shown on the Reedham Tithe Apportionment Map of circa 1840, located in the area 38, marked as 'Cottages and Gardens'. These were a terraced row of 4 cottages, believed to have been built for the workers at the brickworks.

I lived at number 1 cottage with my parents, Joseph and Ellen Williams, from 1947 to 1959 and with my sister Maureen and brother Derek.

The cottages were built of red brick with tiled roofs, and were three storeys high with the top storey being an attic, reached by a ladder. Each of these cottages had two bedrooms on the first floor and downstairs a front room and a back room. No 1 also had a dairy at the back. There was no electric in any of these houses. Mantle and paraffin lamps would be used for light and cooking was done on a coal fire cooking range, upon which the iron was also placed to heat up. Water was collected from the roof into a brick cistern, which we called a well. In the summer months if there had been no rain our father, who worked for 'Yoiton', would collect churns of water from Ashtree farm to top up the well. The clothes were washed in a copper with a coal fire underneath. Originally the coal was delivered by boat and dropped off in a slipway near to Tuck's Mill.

The toilets for these cottages were at the bottom of the gardens and were built of red brick. The 'honeycart' man from Reedham could not get all the way to Berney Arms to empty the toilets and so Henry Hewitt, Yoiton, was paid 5 shillings for each house once a year. The locals buried their sewage and rubbish in the gardens.

These cottages were known to the locals as 'The Barracks'. There was a dyke all the way around these cottages with a wooden bridge at the front, a ligger at the back and another ligger at the side of number 1.

When we started school we had to walk about three quarters of a mile over the marshes, crossing the liggers (planks over the dykes) until we reached the railway line, then over the style onto the railway track and walk to the station. When the weather was wet and muddy we would be soaked, and even with rubber boots on our legs would get muddy. A flannel and towel was brought with us at the ready. The bottom of our coats would get muddy and would not last very long.

There was no shop at Berney Arms at this time and our mother would have a grocery order book and went to Great Yarmouth Tuesdays and Fridays to take her order to Mr Downing, then in Howard Street. He would make up the order and put it in a box and then in his van to take it to Vauxhall Station to be put on the train. On reaching Berney Arms the grocery box would be picked up by father and carried home across the marshes.

One Christmas Eve when we went to Gt. Yarmouth, we usually bought our Christmas tree on this day, it was a lovely sunny morning but while in Yarmouth it began to snow. By the time we got back to Berney Arms it was very bad, and my sister Maureen and myself could not walk any further through the snow, now well above our knees. Father tucked us one under each arm and carried us home across the liggers. After getting home safely father went back out to go and collect the groceries from the station. It was now dark and there was a thick snow blizzard. As he was heading towards the station he could hear someone calling for help. Not being able to see anyone father stood still and called out "Come to my Voice". Eventually the man's voice got nearer as he got to the snow covered ligger he was afraid to cross it so father talked to him and offered an arm till he got across. Father then led him to the station safely but he never did know who the stranger was. Father carried the grocery box to Ashtree farm, where he milked the cows before finally taking the groceries back home to the cottages to get warm by the fire.

Our grandfather Yoiton gave us an old cart, which we kept in the garden. We spent many hours as children playing in it. We had an old bit of canvas cloth for the top and would sit and read our comics here, some days it would be an imaginary car if my brother Derek was about. If our mother was having a cleanout day indoors the mats would be put on the washing line for a bit of air. Sometimes we borrowed them for the cart to make it more comfy.

In 1959 we had to move out to 6/7 cottages as cottages 1 to 4 had been condemned and were to be pulled down.

Figure 27. Left: Mary Ann Eliza Banham (nee Hewitt) with her two oldest children, Francis and Grace, circa 1901. Mary was a daughter of 'King Billy' Hewitt and married Ted Banham. They lived at the cottages and were listed here in the 1901 census. Right: Mary's husband Edward William (Ted) Banham, his father Bob Banham had the Butterfly Mill on the Halvergate Fleet. (C. Carter)

Figure 28. Top: 1 to 4 Cottages in 1928. (M. High). Bottom Left: Ernest, Billy, Betty, Sidney and Norman Hewitt, the children of William and Harriet Hewitt who lived here in the 1920's. Right: Harriet Hewitt with her brother Yoiton, standing, and husband William circa 1920 . (S. Gibbs).

Berney Arms Remembered
SOME OCCUPANTS OF 1 TO 4 COTTAGES

NAMES	APPROX. DATES	NOTES
Cathy Skyoles	1940's	WW11 evacuee. Stepsister to Nora Hewitt at the farmhouse.
William & Harriet Hewitt & family (Ernest, Norman, Billy, Betty & Sid)	1920's.	Harriet was sister to 'Yoiton' and William was his cousin.
Jack and Florrie Farrow & family (Norah, Lilly, Bob & Jack)	c. 1900 to early 1940's	no.1. Son Bob died in WW2.They moved to the railway cottages at 7-Mile. Son Jack moved to Caister and biked every day to 7-Mile to work. Florrie smoked a clay pipe.
Ernest Hewitt, and later with wife Lily and son Tony	1920's & early 1930's	no.2. & 3. 'Yoiton's youngest brother. He left Berney c.1935.
Eliza Hewitt	late 1920's & 1930's	'Yoiton's mother. Widowed in 1927 & moved from the old Inn to no.2. Later moved to station cottages.
Fred High and Millie (nee Hewitt) & family (Janet & Tony)	early 1940's to 1945	no.1. Moved to the house by the New Cut on the Island.
Aubrey Appleton	Early 1940's	no.2. Moved to the bungalow.
Joseph & Ellen Williams & family. (Sheila, Maureen & Derek)	Nov.1945 to 1946 & then 1947 to 1959	no.1. Moved to Raven Hall in late 1946 and returned late 1947 then moved to 6/7 cottages in 1959.
Billy & Elsie Bailey	till 1947	no.2. Billy died 1947.
Albert Hewitt & daughter Violet	1930's to 1947	no.3. Moved to station cottages in 1947.
Jack & Thelma French & family	1952 to 1953	no.2. Moved from & then back to Lockgate Mill Marsh house after floods.

David Pyett and other sailing club members	c.1953 to 1958	No. 2. Used as headquarters and for sleeping sailing club instructors and students during holidays and weekends.
Dick & Liz French & family (Anthony, Richard & Terence)	till 1953	no.3. moved to Yarmouth
James David ('Long Jimmy') & Rose Anna Hewitt (nee Jennis) & family (Millie & Arthur)	1920's till early 1950's	no.4. Rose kept chickens, son Arthur James died in WW2, and Millie married Fred High.
The Easter family	till 1957	no.4.

Janet Church, nee High, remembers being scalded on her legs with boiling water when she lived at no 1. Nurse Jackson from Reedham came out regularly to change her dressings.

Figure 29. From the left James David Hewitt (nicknamed 'Long Jimmy'), his wife Rose Anna (nee Jennis), Ethel Hewitt (a daughter to Albert), Albert Hewitt (James' brother), and Arthur Hewitt, son of James, standing outside the front door to no 4 Cottage. (M. High)

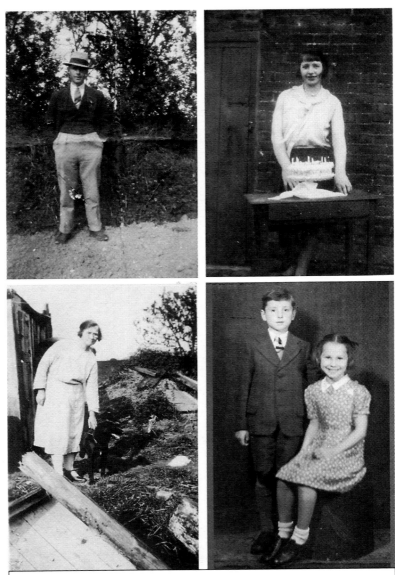

Figure 30. Top Left: Fred High. Top Right: Millie High (nee Hewitt) before she married Fred. Bottom Left: Rose Anna Hewitt, Millie's mother. Right: Tony and Janet High, children of Fred and Millie. (J. Church)

Figure 31. Cottages 1 to 4 in the mid 1950's. Cottage 1 is at the left end of the terrace on the Reedham side. The outside toilet for no 1 is visible on the left of the photograph. (D. Pyett)

Figure 32 Group photograph for the wedding of Billy and Elsie Bailey who lived for a time at no 2 cottage, and showing several people from Berney Arms (M. High).

Standing from left to right: 1 unknown, 2 Mrs Marjorie Juby (nee High) a daughter of marshman James Thomas High and Nellie High once at High's Mill on the Halvergate Fleet, 3 unknown, 4 Billy Runacles from the Berney Arms Station cottages, 5 unknown, 6 Mrs Sarah Runacles from the station cottages, 7 Robbie Mace then living at 6/7 cottages, 8 unknown, 9 Roger Hipperson manager of the Reedham Nursery, 10 unknown, 11 Mrs Ethel Hipperson (nee Hewitt a daughter of Albert Hewitt), 12 Mrs Gertie Farrow then at 6/7 cottages, 13 Albert Hewitt from no 3 cottage, 14 Rose Hewitt (nee Jennis) from no 4 cottage. Sitting from the left: 1 Mr Bailey the groom's father, 2 Mrs Hettie Bailey the grooms mother, 3 Billy Bailey the groom, 4 Elsie Bailey (nee Edwards) the bride, 5 Mary Edwards the brides sister, 6, 7, 8 unknown.

Figure 33. David Pyett and Ken Baker 'Skipper', both sailing instructors, outside number 2 cottage, circa 1955. (D. Pyett)

Figure 34. Short-eared Owl's nest with eggs on the marshes near the Berney station in 1940. (P. Browne). Inset: Short-eared Owl in flight over Berney marshes near cottages. (P. Allard). These owls arrive each winter, usually in small numbers, but sometimes in large numbers. In 1972 Peter Allard found 116 roosting by the Halvergate Fleet.

Figure 35. The Williams family trekking across the marshes from no 1 cottages.

Figure 36. Walking along the railway track and waiting for the train 1953.

Figure 37. Top: Cottages 1 to 4 in the mid-1950's (D. Pyett). Bottom: the site in April 2000 where cottages once stood. This is now referred to as 'the wood' by the RSPB who now own the land. (Hutchinson)

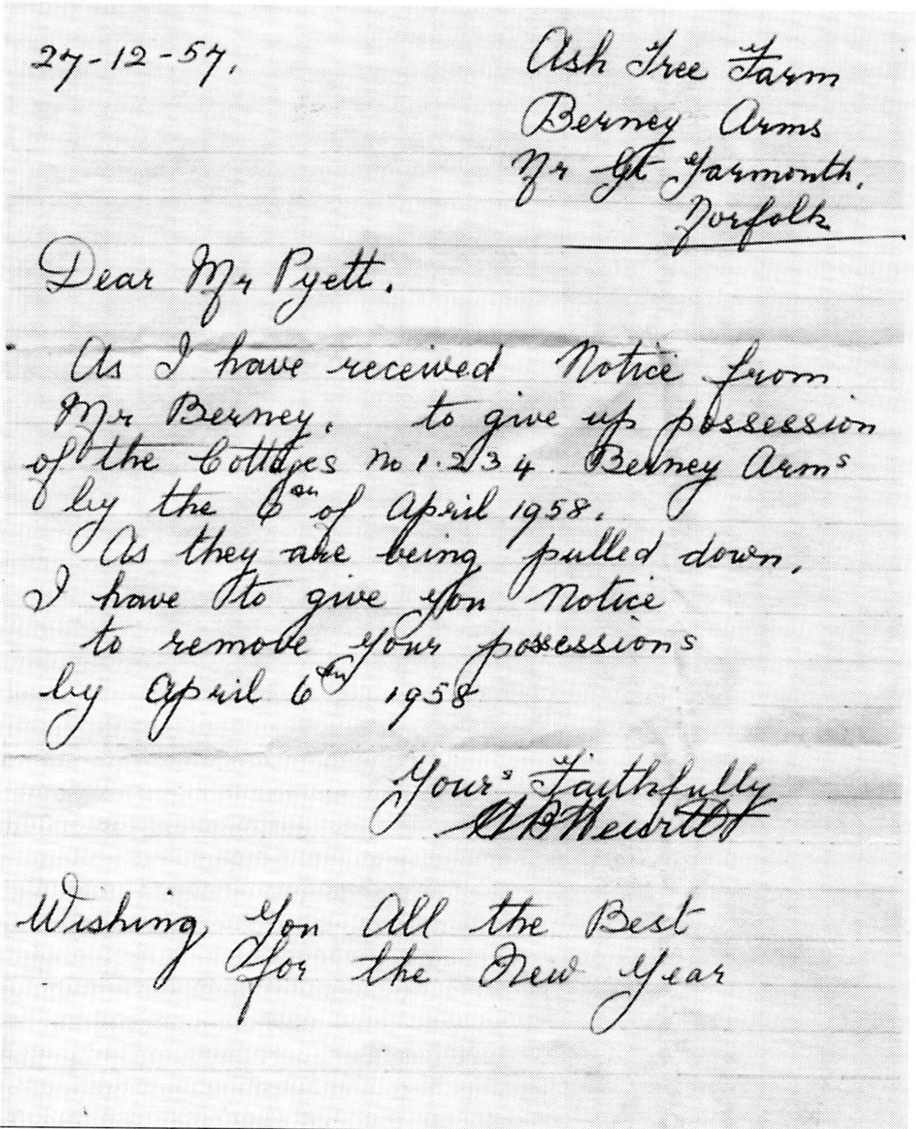

27-12-57.

Ash Tree Farm
Berney Arms
Nr Gt Yarmouth,
Norfolk

Dear Mr Pyett.

As I have received Notice from
Mr Berney. to give up possession
of the Cottages no 1.2 3 4. Berney Arms
by the 6th of April 1958.
As they are being pulled down,
I have to give you Notice
to remove your possessions
by April 6th 1958

Your's Faithfully
H Hewitt

Wishing You All the Best
For the New Year

Figure 38. Letter to David Pyett from Henry Hewitt. (D. Pyett)

Berney Arms Remembered

Thelma French Remembers life at Berney Arms.

My husband John French started work for Mr Harry Hewitt in spring of 1952. Our furniture was taken over the marshes by horse and cart and we moved into No 2 Cottage.

The cottage had an old fashioned oven in the wall and it was the best oven I've ever had, even better than electric ovens. I loved living there, in the summer time sitting on the riverbank watching the boats go by, but when the floods came in 1953 it really frightened me, I was only 22 at that time.

I have several happy memories of Berney Arms and the people who lived there, they were very kind and friendly and would do anything for you, there was only a few people living there but they all helped each other.

My husband used to draw the dykes, that means cutting the reeds etc that were growing in them using a shore knife and a meg. The main dyke ran from Berney to Halvergate, and was seven miles long.

Our neighbours at no 3 Cottage were also called French, but were not relations, but 'Yoiton' used to call my husband and the neighbour Dick the 'French brothers'. Dick French worked in a factory in Yarmouth and when he was on the night shift he used to bring us fresh herring straight off the boats in the mornings. I used to get mushrooms off the marshes and my husband used to shoot the odd rabbit or duck so we were never short of food. I had two children when I lived at Berney and they were both only babies but they use to love watching the boats go by.

Figure 39. Seal basking on the river's edge near 1-4 cottages. (T. Goreham)

ASH TREE FARM (TG464048)

The farmhouse is believed to have been built in 1750-52. It is marked on Faden's map of 1797 and called 'Five mile House'. It is also marked on Wyand's map of 1823, and on the Reedham Tithe Map of circa 1840, where it was shown as area 34, occupied by James Duffield and owned by Thomas Trench Berney. It is also shown on all of the Ordnance Survey Maps since 1883 to the present time as 'Ash Tree Farm'.

It is a redbrick building with a thatched roof. The west part is an extension and housed a chapel on the ground floor. There were various outbuildings, a cart-shed, cowshed and a hay-yard in the 1950's.

There was no electricity here until about 1949 when electric was laid from the new electric pump located near the old mill. My grandfather, Henry Hewitt, 'Yoiton', and nanny, Annie, were living here at the farmhouse at that time. Yoiton did not really want the electric put on, having been so many years without it; but he thought this 'new fangled' stuff was good when a few years later he bought his first television and he could watch the horse racing and wrestling.

The kitchen had a sink with a coldwater tap, the water coming from a spring, also rainwater was collected from the guttering into a water barrel. There was a copper with a fire underneath, which was used washdays, all the washing being put through a big old mangle to get the water out. There was a coal fire cooking range and also, after the electric was put on, an electric cooker.

On the farm Yoiton kept a few cows. They were milked twice a day and the milk churns were taken to the Berney Arms station by horse and cart and put on the train to go to Reedham, where the Milk Marketing Board would pick them up by lorry. This was done every day.

Working on the marshes was hard work and Yoiton employed men to go thistle topping during the summer months, some of the men would help after working all day on the railway. One of these was 'Nutty' Tunget who spent some time at Ashtree farm. In 1946/47 Dan Barber was a cowman for 'Yoiton'.

Yoiton also worked the Berney Pump and the Breydon Pump when pumping was needed.

I often used to go into his woodworking shop with him. One day he was hammering away at this lump of wood and he hit his finger. He called out 'Weelbarrows!' and held his finger. I ran into the farmhouse and asked nanny for a plaster and she say 'You better have two, he might do it agin'.

My sister Maureen, brother Derek, and I would go for tea every Sunday, we usually had tinned salmon and fruit with bread and butter. Granddad's favourite was rice pudding. Jack and Ron Carter, when they were at Berney eel fishing, would take granddad a bucket of eels, granddad loved to cook the eels himself as nanny did not like the smell. He would cook them in a big pan on the electric cooker. The eels, though cut up, would be jumping in the pan and his mouth would be watering. 'Here yar gal. Try some', he say, but they did not appeal to me. When we lived at 6/7 cottage we would go in the summertime for a picnic with nanny, walking along the 'strip' past where 1-4 cottages had

Berney Arms Remembered

stood and then past where Tuck's mill had stood and onto the river's edge near a creek, where we watched the boats and the Golden Galleon go by.

The farmhouse was a large place to keep clean and it was kept spotless. Nanny cleaned the kitchen floor down on her hands and knees scrubbing it. The decorating was done before the summer months when it got busy. Holidays were something not thought about, too much to do in the summer. Nanny and granddad would go to the Norfolk Show together, and Acle Market was the place where a lot of the marsh folk and farmers would meet up. Nanny loved to get out on her coach trips in the summer. She would leave the farmhouse on the horse and cart and get the train to Yarmouth then walk to the seafront to get on the coach – A good day out.

When Stanley Hewitt lived here Mr Berney proposed that the farmhouse should be demolished and replaced with a bungalow. This never happened and the farmhouse was sold eventually to the RSPB who did major renovations.

Figure 40. William Hewitt, 'King Billy', on the left, was the marshman at Ash Tree Farm from about 1885 till 1924. Here he is seen outside the blacksmith's shop at Halvergate next to the Red Lion pub. The blacksmith Mr Beck is second from the right. (S. Gibb)

Figure 41. Outside the Rampant Horse at Freethorpe is 'King Billy' with grandson Bob Hewitt on the cart. Holding the horse is grandson Tom Hewitt and the man standing by the door is believed to be his son-in-law Ted Banham. (S. Gibbs).

Berney Arms Remembered

Figure 42. At the door to Ash Tree Farm house; left, Nora Hewitt, wife of Reggie; centre, her mother Eunice Hewitt, wife of James Hewitt, nicknamed 'Wesmacot'; unknown; and the child at the front is Nora's daughter Linda. (L. Smith)

Micky Hewitt Remembers.

One night in the summer Micky and family went to the Berney Inn. On the way home to the farmhouse they went passed the derelict bungalow and as his mum Barbara climbed a style she saw what she thought was a ghost. They soon realised it was a white Barn Owl.

Micky often went fishing around Berney and caught a nineteen and a half pound pike in the dyke near the Archway gate. He also had a 14 foot long punt in which he would go eel babbing.

When he lived here he got a job at Woolworths in Great Yarmouth, and while working one day he broke a leg. After a visit to the hospital he had a lift by car to Pearson's boatyard at Reedham, where he was taken to Berney by boat. All of this journey he was without his trousers.

Carol Goreham (nee Brackenbury) Remembers.

To visit my grandparents Annie and Henry Hewitt was something of an adventure. After leaving home in the morning, my mum, Ruth; dad, Alan; sister, Brenda and myself walked down to the river at Burgh Castle where my dad rowed us across the river Waveney onto the island. Then it was a walk over planks to cross the reed beds, and then over the marshes to Raven Hall where my uncle Sonny and aunt Barbara lived. After a while there, during which time we would see my cousins Mickey and Cherry, uncle Sonny would row us across the river Yare to Ashtree Farm at Berney Arms where nanny and granddad lived, and had the added bonus of a television set. This was a novelty to us to be able to see 'Watch with Mother' and granddad used to watch horseracing in the afternoons if it was on.

Berney Arms Remembered

We used to explore the cowsheds and see how many swallows nests we could count. Granddad had a working dog called Moss, a ferret, which bit!, a working horse called Hero and lots of cows which I would watch being milked.

Nanny would provide us with dinner and tea and then it would be time for the trek home, but not before nanny had raided the pantry to send us home with the odd tin of peaches or pears and perhaps some of her home-made butter. I loved to help nanny churn the butter. The journey home was slightly different as granddad would take us round to Burgh Castle in his motorboat. We used to make this journey several times during the year and always on Boxing Day. After such an eventful day I was not long getting to sleep to perhaps dream about the next time.

SOME OCCUPANTS OF ASHTREE FARMHOUSE

Name	Approx Dates	Notes
William Hewitt 'King Billy' and family	Circa 1885 till 1924	Marshman / Farmer. He went to live at the old inn for a few years with son Thomas Hewitt before spending his last few months at Wickhampton with daughter Mary Ann Banham.
James David Hewitt 'Westmacot' and wife Eunice Georgina. And son Reggie	1924 till 1946	Marshman / Farmer. A son of King Billy.
Reggie and wife Nora Hewitt		He was Millwright, Carpenter & Wheelwright. Son of 'Wesmacot'. They occupied the west part of the house which became known as 'Noras End'.
Henry Bumbury Hewitt, 'Yoiton' and wife Annie Maria	1946 till 1962	Marshman / Farmer. A grandson of King Billy. After Annie died in 1973 Yoiton returned here to live his last few months with his son.
Stanley Hewitt 'Sonny' and wife Barbara and children Micky, Cherry, Andy, Teresa, and Peter	1962 till 1989	Marshman / Farmer. The son of 'Yoiton'. Remained here for a few years after RSPB took over the house and marshes.
Les & Sheila Street	1986 to 1990's	He was the first RSPB Warden at Berney Marshes. After renovation the house was turned into flats for RSPB members.
Jim Rowe	1990's to present	RSPB employee
Frank Futter	2002 to present	Rents part of the farmhouse.

Figure 43. Top: Henry with grandchildren Maureen and Derek Williams, at the back of farmhouse in 1953 (D. Pyett). Bottom Left: Henry with grandson Andy Hewitt 1955 (B. Hewitt). Bottom Right: Carol Brackenbury with grandmother Annie Hewitt and mum Ruth Brackenbury at front door, c.1959 (C. Goreham)

Figure 44. Annie Hewitt with grandchildren Micky and Cherry in front of Ashtree mid-1950's. (D. Pyett) Bottom: Ashtree Farm in 1969. (P. Allard)

Figure 45. Top: 'Yoiton' photographed in 1959 with son Stanley behind. Bottom: Stanley Hewitt with Berney Mill in the background in 1959. (E. Roberts)

Figure 46. Top: 'Yoiton' talking to the river inspector in 1959. Bottom: Joseph Williams (Paddy) and Stanley Hewitt (Sonny) loading milk churns outside Ashtree Farm to take them to the station 1959. Two churns were from Ravenhall across the river. (E. Roberts)

Berney Arms Remembered

Teresa Leech, nee Hewitt, Remembers

Teresa lived at Ashtree farm from 1962 with her parents Stanley and Barbara, and brothers and sister. She loves horse riding and remembers when she was tiny she would pretend she was riding by using an old oil drum with an old saddle on it. When she was older she rode 'Hero', her granddad's horse. Teresa remembers the day she had on her white trouser suit and high heel shoes to go to Gt. Yarmouth by train. Walking across the marshes she went through a 'cowpat' and decided she had better return home.

After she was married and moved away she would go back to Berney Arms with her daughter Claire by driving down onto the Island and asking her mum to row across the river to collect them. Claire would keep her nanny company at the mill while Teresa rode on her horse for a while.

Figure 47. Teresa Hewitt on Hero at the back of Ash Tree Farm house in the 1960's. (T. Leech)

Charlie Carter Remembers

Charlie is a great grandson of William Hewitt (King Billy). Charlie's father 'Chinky' Carter had an old Ford truck in which Charlie often went with his father. When the people from Berney Arms, The Halvergate Fleet and The Island moved house they would use Chinky's truck.

One of the jobs they used the truck for was to go to Berney Arms to collect Henry Hewitt's muck and take it to Reedham Nurseries.

Chinky sometimes went to the Norfolk show with Yoiton and Annie Hewitt.

One day when Yoiton went to Acle Sale with Chinky, Yoiton bought a young pig and they took it back in the truck to Wickhampton where Joseph Williams, 'Paddy' put it in a sack, slung it over his shoulder and carried it back to Berney to put it in with the stock.

Once in the wintertime Yoiton asked Chinky to order him some pulp. The track was far too wet to travel to Berney so Yoiton asked Chinky if he could store it in a shed for him. "The rats will get it", said Chinky. Yoiton replied, "They want some of it!"

One day Charlie and his father Chinky, with Yoiton's help, were at the Berney station loading railway sleepers onto the truck. As they were lifting one sleeper Yoiton threw his end down and said, "Bloody old pishamire bugger". It was covered in ants.

Figure 48. Chinky Carter's truck. Standing: Charlie Carter, behind the wheel his brother Ivan Carter and on the running board Jip the dog. (C. Carter)

Charlie also remembers Fred Hewitt on the Fleet sold good Ham and that a man came over the marshes to buy some. When the man got it home there was a stone in it, a joke Fred had played on him.

Berney Arms Remembered

John Willimott Remembers

John and Royston Mallett did reed-cutting around the county and out at the Reedham and Berney Marshes. They were self-employed and often did some reed-cutting for Stanley Hewitt on the Island, Reggie Mace, 'Sticher' Gowen and for 'Yoiton'. John and Royston worked together till the 1970's, they would cut 120 bunches a day. In 1953 they were paid half-a-crown (12.5 new pence) a fathom.

'Yoiton' rented the reedbeds at Burgh Castle, Belton and Fritton and the bunches were taken away by wherry.

John and Royston were working on the Island cutting reed for 'Yoiton', one day when 'Yoiton' came across with a Mr Roll, who was buying the reeds from 'Yoiton'. Henry called John over and asked John to bring the bundle he was holding. 'Yoiton' took his pocket-knife out and cut through the string of the bundle and said, 'You are working for Harry Hewitt now, not Sticher Gowen. Make the bundles bigger'. When John and Royston were on their way home they met up with 'Yoiton' and he said 'Don't you make them bunches any bigger, they were big enough as they were.'

In 1953 John and Royston were dyke drawing at Berney Arms on the day of the floods. Yoiton sent Bob Perfect, who was also working for Yoiton, across to them and Bob said, "Harry wants you two". They went to the farmhouse and both were asked to fill sandbags, which had been brought to Berney by the Riverboard and to put them along the quay to help stop the floodwaters.

John and Royston were one day whitewashing the cowsheds for 'Yoiton'. Yoiton came into the shed and seeing John but not Royston said, "Are you on your own John? Where's Jimmy?" There was Royston (Jimmy) standing on the old bull's back whitewashing the ceiling!

Once out at Berney it poured down with rain and was very cold. John was invited into the farmhouse by Annie Hewitt. He took off his rubber boots and when she played the mouth organ he danced around in his stocking feet.

Trevor Dyble Remembers

Trevor worked for the Riverboard for many years up until the early 1970's, and on one occasion when he was working at Berney Arms with Alan Brackenbury, Alan said, 'Let's go for a pint'. Trevor said the pub wouldn't be open at that time of day. Alan said, 'So what. There's no police around here', so they went to the Berney pub. They banged on the door and a small woman let them in. To their surprise standing behind the door was a policeman who was doing his yearly check. They got their pints and the policeman could not do anything because he too was drinking.

The gateways across the marshes needed maintenance to reduce the ruts and prevent mud in the wintertime and 'Yoiton was paid £3 10s 0d per gate whenever there was maintenance required. Trevor drove a bulldozer and 'Yoiton', told Trevor, 'When you go through these gates with your bulldozer rough them up a bit and then you can level them off again later. If you do I'll give you half of what I get paid.' So 'Yoiton' got his money for doing nothing and Trevor got a little money on top of his wages.

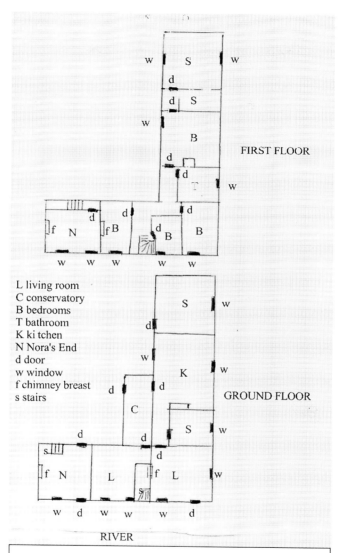

FIRST FLOOR

GROUND FLOOR

L living room
C conservatory
B bedrooms
T bathroom
K ki tchen
N Nora's End
d door
w window
f chimney breast
s stairs

RIVER

Figure 49. Floor plan of Ash Tree Farmhouse in 1980. Not to scale.

Figure 50. Top: Les Street putting up the first RSPB notice boards on Berney Marshes in January 1987. Bottom: Ralph Loughlin, the present RSPB warden for Berney Marshes, in May 1999. (P. Allard)

Figure 51. Ashtree Farmhouse. Top: November 1989 during renovations (Allard). Bottom: April 2000 (Hutchinson)

Figure 52. Top: Michael Seago in 1967 recording Short-eared Owls on Berney Marshes. Bottom: The Seago memorial located near the mill, 2002. (P. Allard). Mr Seago, author of 'Birds of Norfolk' and once president of Norfolk & Norwich Naturalists Society wrote articles for the EDP and helped to conserve the marshes. He died in 1999.

Figure 53. Stanley Hewitt at Ash Tree Farm. Ravenhall and the Langley Detached Mill are in the background. (M. Hewitt)

Figure 54. Sheila being interviewed by Bryan McNerney, 8th June 2001, for 'Riddles of the River' with the Anglia TV film crew. Ash Tree Farm house is in the background and the mill to the left is 'Langley Detached Mill' on the Island.

Figure 55. The Electric pump house and Berney mill in the mid-1950's. Notice the muddy tracks coming from the farmhouse. (Pyett)

Figure 56. Left: Yoiton working inside the Berney pump house in 1959. Right: The electric pump was fed by a temporary electric generator in 2002 while electric lines across the area were being modernised. (Hutchinson)

BERNEY ARMS ELECTRIC PUMP (TG465049)

Housed in a small redbrick building, the electric pump began work in 1949 and took over from the windmill the work of draining the marshes. It had mains electricity brought to it along the river wall from the Breydon Pump. The Berney pump has one 70 horsepower electric motor and can pump up to about 50 tons of water a minute. The pump is now only rarely used as the RSPB keep the water levels high, and any surplus water is taken by the larger Breydon pump.

BERNEY ARMS HIGH MILL (TG465049)

Faden's map 1797 shows a **'Drainage'** mill at this approximate location. This was probably a **cloth-sailed mill**. Patent sails were not invented by William Cubitt till 1807.

Figure 57. The Everard Company's vessel 'Assiduity' in the frozen river in 1947 next to Berney Mill, then in full working order. (P. Allard)

The Norfolk Chronicle 10th Feb 1821 mentions a windmill as part of the Cement / Brickworks so the mill then must be assumed to be grinding the cement clinker. We cannot be certain if it was also draining the marshes. It is quite probable that the cloth-sail windmill had been replaced by a Patent sail windmill by then.

The Norfolk Chronicle 20th April 1822 also mentions that a **Steam Engine** is now part of the cement works. This Steam Engine presumably was built in 1821 as it was not mentioned in February of 1821.

Berney Arms Remembered

Wyand's map of 1823 does not specifically show a mill or a steam engine but shows a 'factory' here. We must assume both a windmill and Steam Engine were part of the factory, while Bryant's map of 1826 shows a **Windmill** and **a Steam Engine** next to Kilns.

Figure 58. Berney Arms Mill in the 1940's in working order. The mill dyke shown here was filled in after the electric pump was used.

The Norfolk Chronicle 13th September 1828 mentions a **Patent Sail Windmill** capable of driving 4 pairs of stones but used for driving circular saws along with a **10hp Steam Engine**. The Norfolk Chronicle 25th June 1836 mentions again both a Patent Sail Windmill and a 10 hp Steam Engine employed for **Sawing, Grinding cement and Draining the marshes.** (It is not clear if the windmill or the Steam Engine or both are used for the marsh drainage but it is probable that both were used for all three jobs.)

The Reedham Tithe Apportionment map circa 1840 mentions 'Factory, Mill and Yards' but does not give details of the mill, and the Norfolk Chronicle 1847 mentions a **5 Storey Patent Sail Windmill** capable of driving 4 pairs of stones along with a **12hp Steam Engine.**

The Norfolk Chronicle 1860 mentions a **24hp Brick Tower** Patent Sail Windmill and a 12 hp Steam Engine both used in the Cement Trade.

The watercolour painting by Charles Harmony Harrison of 1874 shows the windmill with a gallery similar to that which is still present at the third floor and alongside a large building and tall chimney which must be the steam engine building.

The Ordnance Survey map of 1883 shows a **Pumping Windmill** for draining the marshes and a disused Cement factory. Perhaps the Steam Engine is part of the disused facilities. The mill standing today is seven storeys high and, is said to have been built around 1865 by Edward Stolworthy. Whether this was a completely new build, a part rebuild job or simply a hain is not known. Why was it built 7-storey high? Could it simply

Berney Arms Remembered

have been a 'status symbol' to show up against the recently developed Burgh Castle Cement and Brickworks which started about 1859, or could it have been to raise the sails higher above the rest of the adjacent factory buildings so that they caught the wind better?

It is believed that Barnes was the millwright who in 1883 converted the mill to be used for drainage only. The present Berney Arms High Mill is a tarred brick tower mill with an iron stage on the third floor. It is seven floors and stands 70 feet high with an external diameter of 28 feet at ground level and has a boat shaped cap. At the time of writing the mill is undergoing restoration work and is without sails and fantail but it has 4 sails, an 8-bladed fantail, an iron gallery, and a chain pole. The 4 sails were double-shuttered and the span is roughly 80 feet. According to Rex Wailes the sails were not identical, one pair having come from another mill. The scoop wheel, which was used for draining the marshes is 24 feet in diameter and stands separate from the mill. It is encased in a narrow brick-lined culvert and covered with a wooden hoodway. The paddles are eleven inches wide.

After 1883 it was used only as a drainage mill, and would have been worked by the marshmen William Hewitt, ('King Billy'), Jimmy Hewitt, ('Wesmacot') and Henry Hewitt, ('Yoiton'), until 1949 when it was replaced by the electric pump.

The redundant mill was taken over by the Ministry of Public Buildings and Works in 1951 and is now owned by English Heritage.

The sailing club used the mill for a couple of years as their headquarters until renovation work began. When the Ministry of Works began renovating the mill the sailing club rented number 2 cottage which became vacant in 1953. David Pyett and his friends did daring things when they were renting the mill. At one time they fixed a pulley to the fantail of the mill and tied a rope to the handlebars of his bike. David sat on his bike and the others pulled David and the bike up to the mill gallery. David attached a plank of wood to the pilings to make a diving board. One of his tricks was to ride his bike along the rond and then up onto the diving board and into the river. Holidaymakers on the boats would be looking into the river for him to surface. Meanwhile David swam underwater and, out of sight, surfaced and climbed out of the river, walked along the rond and onto the diving board and jumped into the river to fetch his bike. David was a young man a very strong swimmer. The undercurrents in the river Yare are very strong and it is not advisable for anyone to do these things.

The mill was opened to the public in May 1956. During the winter of 1961/2 the mill suffered damage to the sails, fantail and gallery and following this a full restoration was started in 1965 and completed in July 1967. These repairs were carried out by Smithdale and Sons. The mill was overhauled again in 1972/3 and re-tarred and repainted. The mill is currently undergoing more restoration work by Historical Building Conservation Ltd costing about £350,000. The sails were removed in 1999 and the cap of the mill was removed 4th November 2002, repaired, and replaced 6th May 2003. The tower is to be re-tarred and doors and windows repaired during the summer of 2003, and the sails are due to be replaced in September of 2003. Some custodians of the mill since it has been open to the public have been Mr Farrant, Mr Patterson, 'Yoiton', Barbara and Stanley Hewitt, and at the present time Mrs Susan Loughlin.

Figure 59. Berney Mill: left, 1950 (Pyett), right, 1953 (Rackham), Bottom, the scoopwheel in 1965 with from the left, Miss & Mrs Kitchener, Cherry and Teresa Hewitt, Bob Kitchener, and Andy Hewitt. (T. Leech, nee Hewitt)

Figure 60. Top: Peter Hewitt by the scoop-wheel. (B. Hewitt). Bottom: The Berney Mill with stocks but no sails in the 1960's. (M. Hewitt)

Figure 61. Top: Dudley Blake and George Havis, worked for millwrights Thomas Smithdale & Sons, seen here on the fantail extension in the 1960's (D. Havis). Bottom: Stanley and Barbara Hewitt outside the mill. (T. Leech)

Figure 62. Top: Tugboat 'Hector Read', passing Berney Mill on one of her last jobs, towing a crane which is to be used to work on piling at Seven-Mile Reach. Photographed on 18th October 2002. (Allard). Bottom: Removal of the cap from Berney Mill on 4th November 2002. (J. Rowe)

Berney Arms Remembered

Keith Rackham Remembers.
Sailing from Berney Arms in the1950's.

"At Easter 1950 I had my first holiday on the Norfolk Broads, with the Youth Club from Hellesden, Norwich. From then on I was very much into this scene and sailing became a way of life for me at every spare moment. By 1952 the keen ones had the use of the Sea Cadets' 27foot whaler and we were allowed to keep it away from Foundry Bridge, Norwich. We had used it at Barton Broad and then Reedham. This had all been arranged via a Youth Organiser at Norfolk County Council, Ken Baker. He had also obtained the use of the old disused Mill at Reedham that was the Norwich Frostbite's Sailing Club's summer venue. We were in there from around 1951 early 1952. We used to sail from there

Figure 63. View towards Breydon from the top of Berney Mill after the 1953 floods showing the flooded marshes at Burgh Castle. (Rackham)

down to Breydon and Gt. Yarmouth most weekends. Often camping on the marsh overnight. On a Sunday evening it was always a mad rush back to Reedham sometimes having to row quite a way, to get back to the Lord Nelson or the Ferry before closing time.

We had also discovered the Berney Inn by now. The outcome of this was that "Skipper" Ken Baker, got in touch with Mr. Hewitt at the farm and we then moved house, as it were, to Berney Arms. By the summer of 1952 we were camping by the Mill, and keeping our boats in a Dyke near to the farm. The Camping gear and sailing equipment was kept in the Mill.

Whilst all this was taking place we had become instructors on sailing courses that were arranged by the Central Council for Physical Recreation, Bedford. These courses took place at Easter, Whitsun and during the long summer holidays, most of the students were training as teachers, nurses and doctors etc. Some were in their last terms at school. I had my twentieth birthday during January 1953. They were carefree young days.

During late autumn 1952 'Skipper' rented a cottage from 'Partner' Hewitt, which we used for a few weekends, but it was small and we slept in our sleeping bags on the floor or camp beds, without much heating, so before long we moved into the Mill itself there being much more space for our gear. You will have noted that I refer to 'Partner' Hewitt. This is how I always knew him. It had amused Ken Baker, I think, to be addressed as 'Old Partner' by Mr. Hewitt. I, having been brought up on a farm at Ringland, during the war, was used to this form of address. Therefore I always referred to Harry as Partner Hewitt.

Figure 64. 'Lady Marjorie', a Thames sailing barge built in 1893, photographed in the early 1950's from the Berney Mill. (Rackham)

During the summer of 1953 we had obtained permission from the Ministry of Works to use the Mill as a base for the summer sailing course. The CCPR provided hammocks and cork filled palliasse for the use of the boys who would sleep at the mill. Muriel and Dick who at the time were running the Inn provided accommodation for the girls. The Inn also produced the meals and evening entertainment with the odd talk on sailing theory thrown in for good measure.

I was an apprentice at Mann Egerton, Cromer Road, and could not therefore spend all the summer as a course instructor, however I was there at weekends and sometimes during an evening. Getting there was the challenge.

Berney Arms Remembered

The recognised way was by train, an alternative was to cycle to Reedham and then by devious means get on to the track and cycle alongside to Berney Arms, not without its hazards as you will know, trains being the least of them. Clinker, large stones, and

Figure 65. Sailing club members having a wash by the brick culvert at Berney in early 1950's. (Rackham)

signal wires etc; have a habit of creeping up on you when in a guilty hurry. I think it was sometime around September, perhaps 1952,that I decided one Friday evening I would cycle to Wickhampton and find my way over to the Mill from there. I had of course seen 'Partner' Hewitt cycling about his areas of marsh and zipping over the 'liggers' across the dykes. (Not that I intended to ride over myself). I also recall that 'skipper' told a tale of one Friday afternoon, when he had left work early and gone to Berney for the weekend he saw 'Partner' having a set too with a bullock that had got a bit frisky with him. 'Partner' set about it with his stick and drove it backwards into a shallow dyke, telling it, 'That will cool you off, you young bugger'. I had no intention of emulating this antic either.

Suffice to say that I started out from Wickhampton on a fairly well defined track and negotiated several marshes without any problem. Then the track became less well marked, in fact not really marked at all. I found my way into several more marshes and went around the edges until I could cross into the next one. All the time aiming for the Mill which one can see quite easily. I have always believed in straight lines maybe that's where I went wrong! I could eventually see the station and crossing gates, by now it was just about dark, I was some way 'downstream' as it were, but not far out. I then got into a marsh that had no outlet towards my destination. Out of the gloom came some interested young cattle, don't ask me, I didn't stop to check. The dyke wasn't too wide, so I threw my Bergen rucksack, then my bike and myself into the next marsh, only to discover that more interested young cattle were there awaiting my arrival. Now having spent from the age of 8 until 16 living on a farm, and being involved with milking cows from about the age of 12, I wasn't too fussed about being followed around as I looked for a way off the marsh. I couldn't find one, nor could I find a 'ligger'.

The dyke between me and the mill was somewhat wider than the last one but not impossible, I hoped. Somebody behind was getting a bit friendly with my bike so I turned around and tried to get them to go away, they did for a yard or two, but by the time my Bergen was across the dyke they were within range again, snuffling my bike. Shooed them off and slung the bike across. Then it was a short bull/heifer fight before I legged at the dyke as hard as I could in an effort to get over. I made the opposite bank, body-wise, but one leg/foot trailed into the water and I was somewhat wet from the waist down. I crawled out and was within a few yards of the railway fence. I walked to the crossing and made it to the mill somewhat dampened and disillusioned about any cross country route to the mill. I never tried it again, preferring river, rail or trackside to bull fights.

On the sailing side of things I well remember the day I had about six people out in the whaler, on Breydon, I had explained to them that we had to keep within the marker posts to be in the deepwater channel. But a naval whaler, being a ships boat, is frequently rowed to go ashore, and therefore has a retractable centre plate. When the tide is right and the wind favourable one can sometimes cut across part of the 'dog Legs' on the inside to make straighter passage. So we proceeded to try same. Somebody stands by on the centre plate which we had set half up, to get it full up if needed. We skimmed around the back of one post and maybe another and then headed for a bigger short cut, about a third of the way down Breydon. We then felt the boat drag across some mud then carry on, Then the bow grounded, the drill was carried out, up plate spill the wind. I nipped forward and stepped over the side to push off. When I looked up I have never seen so many people with expressions of shock and disbelief on their faces as my six crewmates. I pushed off, they got sailing again and I hung over the side to wash off my feet and legs, almost helpless with laughter. It took them several moments to realise that if the boat runs aground there's not too much water under the bow, and in tidal waters you need to get off fast if you can. They saw the chap in charge getting off the boat in the middle of acres of water and leaving them to their fate. That was part of that evenings entertainment.

Dave Pyett and I spent a lot of time at the Mill all the year round, he brought an old bike there and we had goes at riding it around the balcony, I don't recall that we ever made it all the way around, I certainly never did, the wheels slid into the gaps and had us off.

Skipper got the bright idea that we could do a bit of abseiling. So we tied rope to the mill shaft led it out of the balcony door and proceeded to climb up and down a few yards.

We thought nothing of clearing snow out of the whaler before going for a sail during the colder days of winter. We also got along to the mill fairly soon after the 1953 floods, during January, to find out how our boats had got on, they were OK. I took a few photographs of the flooded marshes from the top of the mill and I guess we may have gone for a short sail, providing the tide was right.

What I do remember is that one late afternoon when the tide was fairly racing out, a hired cabin cruiser came down river with the intention of mooring. The helmsperson tried to run alongside near the mill, the boom promptly started bouncing off most of the piling uprights and the tide and wind just took the craft and the panic stricken crew on down to Breydon at breakneck speed. We never did know what became of them. We also caught sight one weekend of a small motor cruiser that had moored upriver a short way, on the opposite bank, obviously on a high tide. They had a rude awakening at some time when a submerged pile had come up through the cockpit floor and others had emerged outside the boat trapping it near the bank. Such was life on the river during the 1950's.

When I arrived one Friday evening, Skipper had been there since the Thursday and he had borrowed a gun and been duck shooting, therefore that weekend we had duck as our main course. Our cooking was done on Primus stoves so it would have been stew, with vegetables thrown in. By the end of Sunday it would have degenerated into a soup style gumbo with all the leftover bits in the one big saucepan. One just hoped that nothing too distasteful came out on your plate when it was served up."

David Pyett Remembers.

"I first met that grand old man of the marshes Harry Hewitt, when as a member of the Mill Sailing Club as we named ourselves, had to leave Reedham Mill, which we rented from the Norwich Frostbite Sailing Club, when they had an offer for it they couldn't refuse. We had admired Berney Mill on our trips down to Breydon water, now we needed a new base. Enquiries were made and we were pointed to Ash Tree Farm and, a Mr, Harry Hewitt. What a character: full of life and laughter. Having explained our situation he said, "You leave that to me old partners, I'll sort that out for you."

A month later we were in residence, but the key had to be collected and returned to the farm. Prior to moving in we sailed down one weekend and pitched tents on the marsh by the mill. Having a brew up, Harry joined us and looked over the camp. "I see you haven't put a snake ring down", he said. "What's that?" we asked. "Snakes won't go over rope", he said, "That will keep you safe." We spent the next hour stripping the running and standing rigging off the boats to encircle the tents. Next day he asked if we had seen any snakes. We told him no. "There you are then, that works." It was the first time he had us going and, certainly wasn't the last.

Berney Arms Remembered

Within a year the Ministry of Works, acquired the mill as an ancient monument and, spent £3,000 renovating it. Harry let us move all our gear into his sheds. The Ministry let us move back in as resident caretakers. Having moved a lot of the gear back

Figure 66. Top: Golden Galleon and Bottom: 'Lady Sonia', both photographed from Berney Mill in early 1950's. (Pyett)

one afternoon, it was dark when I returned the key to Harry. On the way this dark figure loomed up walking towards me, I said good evening but had no answer, I turned and watched it disappear into the night wondering who on earth it could be. When I mentioned it to Harry he said, "You've seen the black lady". It seems that nuns lived in a chapel that was built into the farmhouse long ago, and that this was a well known ghost. At the time I thought Harry was having me on again, but his lovely wife Annie assured me it was true.

Another evening when I arrived to collect the key he said, "You can't go yachting tomorrow the tides are wrong, and I want you to come with me to Burgh Castle to nut some pigs". He always tried to improve my education. One day on arriving I decided to go the back way over the marsh as it had been wet and, the track near the farm would have been knee deep in mud. I was wearing a duffel coat with a large coil of rope over one shoulder, and a holdall, full of tins of soup plus vegetables and spuds in my hand. Looking round for mushrooms I saw Harry's bull coming at the gallop. I took off at full speed knowing there was a main dyke ahead with a ligger crossing it, which is a heavy plank about a foot wide. My fear was whether I would have the three or four seconds needed to slow down in order to step on the ligger. No problem, the ligger had been moved! I took off in full flight thinking I was in for a swim, but landed many feet beyond the dyke, still hanging onto the rope and bag. I'm sure to this day I must hold the unofficial record for the long jump. I complained to Harry the next day, he raised an eyebrow and said, "Next time old bull comes after you, just you lie down". "Why?" I asked, expecting to hear some ancient country lore. "That save him the trouble of knocking you down."

The memory I shall never forget was going down to work on a boat a Thursday in late January. Crossing from the station I noticed the levels of the dykes were lower than usual. The drainage pump by the mill was working away. I mentioned this to Harry and he said, "I'm emptying the dykes." I asked him why. "There's going to be a tempest and I don't want the marshes flooded." On the Saturday night the east coast flooded causing hundreds of deaths. The met office gave warnings only after it began to flood. How he knew three days ahead I never could discover.

Harry was a master of economics. Arriving one day I noticed something odd by his mooring. Going over it was a table and a sign reading "Marsh Hares 2/6"; having paunched and skinned hundreds of rabbits I was mystified. On seeing Harry I asked what they were. "Coypu" he said, "they must be good, one gentleman going up to Norwich bought one. That was so good he bought another on his way back." There was a plague of them at that time and, the ministry paid a shilling a tail plus a replacement cartridge. Harry used to net some of the coypu and said, "my duck shooting don't cost nothing". He saw me with a sheldrake one day and asked what I was going to do with it. "It's going to be our meal tonight" I replied, "Well" he said, "make sure you put a housebrick in the oven at the same time as old bird". "Why is that?" "When that brick is fit to eat, so will the bird". How right he was. He truly was the most unforgettable character I've met and a real gentleman. "

Figure 67. Top Wherry 'Albion', built in 1898 and renovated in 1949, sailing past Berney Arms in mid 1950's, bottom sailing club at Berney Arms. (Pyett)

Figure 68. 'Sociality', a Dutch built dry cargo vessel, owned by F T Everard of London, photographed from Berney Mill in the early 1950's. (Pyett)

Figure 69. Top: Dutch motor vessel 'Metropole' photographed at Berney Arms in May 1962 (Allard) Bottom: 'Appleby' returning from Cantley passing Berney Arms in October 2000. (Hutchinson)

Figure 70. Flood defence work at Berney Arms. Top: ground anchor coils awaiting use, 28 April 1998. Bottom: drilling rig installing anchors and backfilling between new & old piles, 17 February 1998. (Flowers)

Berney Arms Remembered
RECENT FLOOD DEFENCE WORK AT BERNEY ARMS

Tilbury Douglas were engaged by the Environment Agency to install new steel sheet piling along 575 metres of river frontage between Ashtree Farm and Berney Arms public house. The old piling was in a very poor state and had reached the point where it could have collapsed at any time, resulting in the collapse of the flood bank and flooding of the marshes. The work was carried out in 1998 and completed in June 1999 at a cost about £2,000,000.

The water is deep along the frontage, and as a result the steel sheet piles used were 15 metres long. To stop them falling over they had to be 'anchored' at the top. This was done using a technique called Ground Anchors. A hole is bored through the piles and under the ground. Into this hole is inserted steel cable within a flexible plastic sleeve. Cement grout is then pumped into the sleeve so that it expands. When the cement has set, this forms a solid plug with the cable in the centre. A hydraulic jack is then used to tighten the cable and pull the piles tight against the bank. It is then fixed in place with a cap or 'wedge' to lock it in position so that the jack can be removed. This is a complicated and costly method, but it has the major advantage that all the work can be done from the rivers edge avoiding the need to dig up fields so that an anchor can be installed. The ground anchors used at Berney Arms were about 30 metres long so you can imagine the potential mess if they had dug trenches instead.

This is the work being carried out in the two photographs. The coils stored on the bank in the photograph with the Windmill are the Ground Anchors described above.

In the photograph with the Berney Arms pub is the drilling rig installing the anchors. This is on the floating pontoon in front of the crane. You can see the angle at which the anchors are being placed. The small excavator in the foreground is simply backfilling behind the piles. You can see the new line of piles in front of the old one.

RSPB WINDPUMPS

There are at present six small pumping windmills on the RSPB Berney Marshes reserve. These are used, mostly in the summer months, to pump water from the dyke system onto designated small low lying areas of marshland to create ideal conditions for wading birds and wildfowl. All were specially designed by the RSPB, and installed by them. The first became operational in April 1995 pumping water onto the 'Seago' main flood. They all have a small turbine pump and have proved quite a success. The last one, the tallest and the most powerful began work in spring of 2002 actually pumping water from the Halvergate Fleet dyke onto the northern sections of the reserve. A powerful electric pump situated by the Fleet dyke is occasionally used in summer if the water levels are unusually low. There are three in the south section of the reserve, two in the northern areas and one on the Wickhampton side of the marshes.

Figure 71. Top, left: The First RSPB skeleton windpump 25-4-1995, right: The Second pump 8-4-1997. Bottom, left: The East pump erected in 1999, 25-6-2002, right: The North pump erected 16-4-2000 and photographed 6-4-2000. (Allard)

Figure 72. Top left: Wickhampton RSPB skeleton windpump, 30-5-2002, bottom left: RSPB pump near the site of Goffin's mill with Howard's House in background, erected 14-2-2002, photo 6-4-2002. (Allard). Right: Ralph Loughlin RSPB warden working on a skeleton windpump, 5-8-1998 (Flowers).

Berney Arms Remembered

CEMENT WORKS (TG465049)

Between the mill and the bungalow there was once a cement works and sawmill. The bungalow and mill were in fact part of these cement works, and the cottages at Berney Arms were probably built to accommodate the workers. Between the cottages nos 6/7 and the inn there was also a brickfield. Since the river was the main form of transport before the invention of the steam engine, and there was a good local supply of lime from Whitlingham and clay from Breydon and Oulton Broad it is easy to see why a factory would be built here by the river.

Norfolk Chronicle, 13 September 1828:
'REEDHAM CEMENT WORKS
Sawing Mills, Brick & Tile Kilns.
To be Let For a Term of Years, with Immediate Possession,
At Reedham in the County of Norfolk.
A Well Established CONCERN situate at the junction of two Navigable Rivers, near the Sea Port Town of Great Yarmouth, consisting of a Kiln, manufactory, ten horse steam engine, extensive warehouses, counting room, quay, roomy yard and two cottages for workmen. Also a very powerful Windmill with patent sails, driving seven circular saws and a deal frame particularly adapted for Sawing for Herring Barrels, in which a very considerable trade is now carried on. The Windmill is capable of being converted to any other Trade requiring great power, as it is built to draw four pairs of Stones. Also a capital Tile Kiln with extensive and well arranged tile sheds, two Brick Kilns with spacious grounds adjoining, coal bins and other requisite buildings, four good cottages for workmen; an unlimited supply of fine Brick and Tile earths upon the premises.
A Comfortable Residence with or without 150 Acres of fine Grazing Land may be hired with the above.
Apply to Messrs. Woodrow & Newton, Norwich. (Letters to be post paid). Principals only will be treated with.'

Norfolk Chronicle, 3 March 1860:-
'THE REEDHAM CEMENT WORKS driven by Steam and wind power near Yarmouth.
TO BE LET for a term of years.
They consist of a 12-horse steam-engine and a 24-horse brick tower patent sail wind mill late in the occupation of Mr. Reynolds, in the cement trade, situate at the mouths of the Norwich and Beccles rivers with water communications to most parts of Norfolk and Suffolk. The Berney Arms Station on the railway from Yarmouth to Norwich, London and the north is within five minutes walk and a tram road to the same may be laid at small expense. The situation is well calculated for the manufacture of Portland cement, being in the immediate neighbourhood of an inexhaustible supply of the best materials for making the same.
Apply to Mr. Nesbitt, Morton near Norwich.'

Great Yarmouth Mercury, 2 April 1866:-
'John Milligan age 20 of Berney Arms Cement Works drowned in the Haven Gt. Yarmouth and body was picked up on Good Friday'

The Burgh Castle Cement Company occupied the Berney Arms works from the early 1870's. The Berney Arms works were eventually closed down about 1880 but the mill continued to grind clinker which was transported by wherry to Burgh Castle until 1883, after which time the mill was used as a drainage mill.

Berney Arms Remembered

Some of the Berney Arms cement works buildings stood for several years after closure of the factory, and Ernest Hewitt recalls that his father Thomas Edward Hewitt used one of the old cement works kilns as his blacksmith shop into the 1920's.

The last remains of the cement kilns were bulldozed down about 1950 and the rubble was used to fill the old dyke leading to the mill which was no longer required after a new dyke had been cut to the new electric pump. A few bits of rubble, however, are still present to this day.

Figure 73. Top: the cement works as painted in 1874 by Charles Harmony Harrison. Bottom: the remains of the cement works around 1900. (R. Malster). Cottages 6/7 are seen on the right in both pictures.

Berney Arms Remembered

BUNGALOW (TG465050)

The bungalow was built of grey bricks with a slate roof and was probably originally built as an office for the cement works. The large windows faced the cement works. It was, however, also lived in, as the censuses show.

For a few years around 1900 when Isaac Hewitt, the millwright, lived here his wife Emma used the parlour as a nursery school for the local children who later went to the school at Reedham.

Some Occupants of the Bungalow

Name	Notes
Isaac & Rose Emma Hewitt & family	From before 1891 – He was a son of King Billy and was a Millwright. He used the brick shed at no 6 cottage as his store & workshop. The Parlour was used as nursery school for the Berney children. They moved to Reedham
Reggie &Blanche Mace & family	1930's till 1945 when they moved to Seven-Mile house
Aubrey Appleton & Denis Robertson	Bought it from Berney Estate in mid 1940's
Mr & Mrs Archie & Violet Hitchcock	From 1953 to early 1960's
Mr Baker	Circa 1963 - made a spring & capped it
Mr Bob Manning	Bought & demolished the bungalow circa 1969 while he had the pub.

Ivan Mace whose family lived here recalls it had a large room facing the river, which was sectioned off to make two bedrooms, a bedroom facing the station, a big parlour facing the mill, a kitchen facing the mill and a living room facing the station. A wooden toilet was down the garden under an oak tree.

After Mr Manning left the marshes he kept possession of the plot where the bungalow had stood and still owns it today.

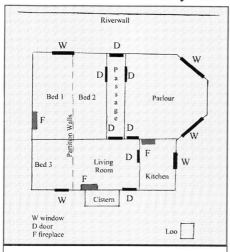

Figure 74. Floor plan of bungalow from Ivan Mace. (Not to scale).

Figure 75. A young Reggie Mace in 1926.

Figure 76. View, from the Berney mill, of the bungalow and 6/7 cottages in the snow in mid-1950's. (D. Pyett)

Figure 77. Left: View of Cement works ruins and bungalow from the mill in early 1950's. Right: Members of sailing club in front of the bungalow in early 1950's. (D. Pyett).

Berney Arms Remembered
David Schwartz Remembers

I was about seven years old when I visited my grandparents Violet and Archie Hitchcock just after they moved into the Bungalow in 1953. Soon after they bought a lovely black Labrador called Pip. I used to spend all my holidays with them. Later my Uncle Laurence Davis and his wife Dianne bought the Red mill next to Ravenhall. Their children Graham and Ginette were regular visitors. When I was very young and Charles Schofield had the Berney Inn, I think it was over the Christmas holiday we had a very disturbing experience. It was about seven o'clock one cold winters night when my mother Iris, Violet Hitchcock, my cousin Lisa and I walked along the fields to the Pub with only a torch to see by. The Schofields and us were sitting alone in the room facing the river. There was nobody else at all anywhere near the inn. It was about 8.30 pm when the lights started to flicker. We couldn't understand why. The next minute we heard a creaking sound and we all looked towards the door. We watched in amazement as the door handle slowly turned and the door suddenly flung itself open. We were petrified. As I was so young they told me to stay put as Charles and my cousin went outside to look around. They found nothing and came back. A few minutes later during the excitement my mother looked out of the window and gave a shout. Gliding along the bank about 30 feet from us was a hooded figure all wrapped round in a long flowing smock. Its head was bowed against the wind and it had an oil lamp in it's hand. It strode along the bank for a few yards until it came to a style that was there then. At that point a second figure appeared, similar to the first and followed the first one. We were all in a state of shock. At that point the first one proceeded to pass straight through the style and then disappeared. The second one went through the style and disappeared. Someone stayed with me and the rest went searching the bank for signs of footprints. Nothing was found. We went straight back to the bungalow in a tight bunch. My grandfather Archie thought we were all mad and said we had imagined it. I can remember vividly going to bed that night on my own in the bedroom facing the bank of the river. I was very nervous. The next night my grandfather and my uncle Ronnie who had arrived at the bungalow earlier that day went down to the Inn determined to find out from the Schofields what had happened the night before. While they were chatting about it in the same room as us the previous night the same thing happened again, the same two apparitions! To put it mildly we were astounded. They appeared again for a further three nights, a total of five appearances. The story appeared in the Norfolk press.

To my knowledge they were never seen again. However, there have been many sightings of a little old man at the entrance to the cellar before it was all changed. I believe both Ken Barnes and Bob Manning have seen him.

A few years later I remember when Sheila and her brother and sister Derek and Maureen moved in next door. I can remember being taken for a special treat for a boat ride on the river by Jack Hunt. I can recall that he had a very strange laugh. We all thought it very funny. He used to pop in a lot. In fact he took my Grandmother to Reedham in his boat when she was taken ill. She later died and Archie came back to live with his son Raymond in London. Pip the Labrador came too. Before all that, I can recall waiting for Henry Hewitt to come along with his horse and trap. As he came past the Berney Mill he would stop and wait for me to jump on and I would go with him to the station to drop off the milk churns. Over the years I would always chat to Stan and Barbara Hewitt when they looked after the mill. I remember Bob and Violet Mace, they were the first people I would meet when I got off the train.

Over the years long after the Bungalow was sold I stayed at Langley Detached Mill (Red Mill as we knew it). Then after my Uncle sold it I hired boats and moored up outside the Berney Inn or the Mill and I return almost every year. Then I got married and brought my children down too. They have never believed my stories about the Ghosts even after my mother backed me up. Anyway I am hiring a boat again with my wife Ruth this May and I am so looking forward to meeting Sheila Hutchinson after all these years.

6/7 COTTAGES (TG465051)

These semi-detached cottages were built of red brick with a tile roof. Each cottage had two bedrooms upstairs and a kitchen and living room downstairs. On the side of the building nearest to the bungalow it had two brick built sheds adjoining number 6. When I lived here the two houses had been converted into one and the sheds were used one as a work-shed and the other a play-area. There was no electric; mantle lamps and candles were used for lights. There was no running water. The water was collected from the roof into a brick-lined cistern. Cooking was done on a coal-fire cooking range and there was a copper with a coal-fire underneath in one of the backrooms and this was used for washing. The toilet was a wooden hut outside and was emptied regularly.

We lived here till 1963 and shortly afterwards the cottages were pulled down. Some of the previous occupants here were Stanley High in the 1920's, Blanche Hewitt, Elsie Bailey, Billy and Gertie Farrow, Allen and Ruth Brackenbury, and Ralph and Elvira Hunt and family.

Figure 78. Ernest Hewitt and Walter Edwards, known as Farrow, in the late 1920's. Walter lived with the Farrows at 6/7 and suffered from TB. He had a rotating wooden hut put up nearby that always faced the sun. (I. Mace)

Derek Williams Remembers.

One of my earliest memories of Berney is when my mother, Ellen Williams, sisters Sheila and Maureen, and I were leaving the farmhouse where my grandmother, Annie Hewitt lived. As my sister Sheila turned to wave goodbye she walked straight into a dyke. Mother rushed over and pulled her out. I wasn't sure what she smelled of so I didn't get too close to her on the way home.

One Christmas I got a metal pedal car which I spent many happy hours playing in, but I probably spent as much time repainting it. I would ask grandfather, 'Yoiton' if he had any old paint, then rush home to start work. My mother must have spent as many hours cleaning up a six year old boy and his clothes.

Later I recall riding with father, Joseph Williams, on the cart taking grandfather's milk across the marshes to the station, and how pleased I was to hold the reins on the return trip, even though the horse knew the trip much better than me.

One day my sister Maureen, Kavan Hunt and myself lit a small fire in part of the old brickwork ruins. Then we saw grandfather's cart coming, thinking to save us from

Figure 79. No 6/7 cottages in the early 1950's. (Pyett)

getting into trouble, Kavan sat on the fire to try to hide it. Grandfather passed by without mentioning the fire or the smoke so we were out of trouble, but I never did know the state of Kavan's trousers.

Some days I would fish for eels in the river. I was all right until it came to putting the worms on the hook. I couldn't bear to pick them up, so I got Sheila to do it as she was so much older and braver than me. One time father joined me but he used a line with several hooks, which he just threw into the water. All went well until he forgot to tie the other end to something. When he threw the hooks in he lost the lot. I found some new words that day.

Another favourite pastime in summer was sitting by the river talking to the holidaymakers, giving them our own version of the history of Berney Arms: one day it would be King Arthur's knights, another time it would be the Normans trying to build castles. We even convinced some that there used to be a tunnel leading from Reedham Church to Berney mill, then going under the two rivers to Burgh Castle. The people often gave us a few coppers for sweets, but I can imagine the confusion if different sets of people met up later and compared stories.

When we lived at 6/7 cottages and our neighbour's relations visited each year we would play cricket beside the bungalow. We would play after tea but with only about six players the game would come to a sudden stop when the older players ran indoors at 6.45 to listen to the 'Archers' on the wireless.

One snowy winters day Sheila returned from a trip to Yarmouth. We knew that she usually brought some cream cakes home. Maureen and I blocked the path with a forty-gallon drum, stacked up snowballs behind it, and when Sheila tried to pass we said she couldn't till she gave us a cake. She refused so we started throwing snowballs at her until

Berney Arms Remembered

mother heard the noise and came charging to the rescue. She looked a sight, headscarf done up like a turban, curlers sticking out, waving a broom at us. We made ourselves scarce until things quietened down then went indoors; I think we did get our cakes later but whether we deserved them I'm not sure.

We got into another scrape that summer when we were playing with an old bit of rope while mother was hanging out her washing. She stood near the linen post and we circled her with the rope and she ended up tied to the post. The louder she shouted for us to let her go the more scared we got to untie her so we went and hid on the marshes. I think Sheila let her free but I've never been sure.

A favourite hiding place for us children was our old dog's kennel, which was really a forty-gallon drum on its side. We would pull out the poor dog, Moss, crawl in, then pull the dog back in before he had a chance to know what was happening. With him in front of you nobody could ever see you. If the dog was awake he seemed to enjoy the company and thought it was a good game. God bless you dear old Moss, we did it often enough.

Once as I finished a drink of water I asked what to do with the remainder in the cup as water was scarce in the summer. "Put it anywhere", I was told, so I did. Maureen was leaning forward reading and the gap between her collar and neck was too much temptation, so that's where I put it. Move over Moss here I come again!

Time spent indoors was usually only in very bad weather and was occupied by board games and jigsaws and comics etc. I loved to set up my battery operated train set and would spend hours with it, but sadly, as money was tight, batteries were considered a luxury item and it seemed I had to wait forever to get new ones

Figure 80. Derek Williams at Berney circa 1959. (D. Williams)

I think the most lasting memory of Berney Arms is when we were at 6/7 cottage and I was given my own bedroom at the back and I could look out of the window and see for miles: grandfather's cows would be grazing nearby, trains on the Berney line, more marshes with cattle grazing, Wickhampton church, trains on the Acle line, and cars on the Acle New Road in the distance. I would imagine that some people would pay hundreds of thousands of pounds for a view like that today! Sadly when the first heavy rain came the roof leaked so badly that I had to join my sisters in their room.

Just after my eleventh birthday we left the marshes and I was heartbroken. I enjoyed the life, which was tough at times but had many lighter moments. I'm just glad I had the chance to experience that kind of lifestyle.

Figure 81. The Riverboard doing some repair work to the piling at Berney Arms between the cottages and the inn in 1953, sometime after the floods. (C. Goreham)

Berney Arms Remembered

BERNEY ARMS INN (TG468052)

The inn was probably built in the eighteenth century although it was not marked on Faden's map of 1797. It does appear on all subsequent maps. It was a public house until 1909 when it lost it's licence and became a farmhouse. By about 1943 the building was in a bad state of repair and it was left vacant for a few years. The Inn belonged to the Berney family estate until they sold it in about 1947 to Aubrey Appleton and Denis Robertson. After a time they sold it to Mr Matthews who repaired the pub and put on a new roof. The Matthews had a septic tank built and a spring was made inside the old inn to provide running water. The spring was bored by well-borers Buckenham of Hethersett. The Matthews opened the place as a guesthouse and they collected guests from the Berney Arms station with a pony and trap.

Later after the pub changed hands a small shop was added. Getting staff for the pub and shop has been a problem ever since the cottages were pulled down and there was no one else left living locally, except at the farmhouse. Getting to the pub to go to work, for someone coming from elsewhere, is quite a problem as the trains are infrequent and at inconvenient times, and the track from the Acle New Road has not always been easy to cross in a car. 'Live-in' staff have been employed since Mr Manning took over the pub.

The owner at the time of the Reedham Tithe Apportionment circa 1840 was Thomas Trench Berney. His eldest son George Duckett Berney inherited the estate. He then died without any descendants and his eldest surviving nephew George Augustus Berney inherited.

It should be noted that the occupier as listed in various documents was not always resident at the pub. William George for example was listed as 'occupier' in the Tithe Apportionment but was not a resident of Reedham in 1841 but he was also listed in 1836 as licensee of the Reedham Lord Nelson. Also Charles Knights, listed in the 1864 and 1868 directories as the victualler, was not a resident. He was at that time the owner of Hobland Hall and his brother James was in residence at the pub.

The pub was leased by the brewery Steward & Patterson in about 1875 and when it regained its licence it became a freehouse.

Ernest Hewitt Remembers

Ernest Hewitt was born in 1910 at the Berney Arms Inn and he lived here with his parents Thomas and Eliza, and his older brothers and sisters. Ernest tells the tale how Reggie Mace, Walter Farrow (Known as Farrow but correct surname was Edwards) and himself closed all the windows and doors to the bungalow and tied one door shut but forgot the front door. They climbed onto the bungalow roof and put a slate on top of the chimneypot. The smoke filled the bungalow and Isaac Hewitt, the millwright living there at the time, came rushing out coughing and spluttering in a rage and chased after them. Ernest's grandfather was the marsh-farmer William Hewitt, 'King Billy', who lived at Ash tree farm when Ernest was a youngster. A trick Ernest used to earn some spending money was to put a cow in a dyke and make sure it could not get out, and then he would go and tell his grandfather that a cow was in a dyke. Ernest would be paid for the information and paid again for helping to pull the animal out of the Dyke.

When a body was found in Breydon it was laid out in the mill. Occasionally Isaac Hewitt the millwright would make a coffin and the relatives would come and pick up bodies by boat or more often by train.

E.D.P. 11 February 1955:-
'New Licence for Berney Arms Inn
Was Wherrymen's Public-House

After 50 years the Old Inn, Berney Arms, the former wherrymen's public-house is to be licenced to sell liquor again. At Blofield and Walsham Brewster Sessions on Monday the Bench granted a licence subject to confirmation to Mr. Charles Leslie Schofield to sell beer, wine and spirits off the premises.

In his application Mr. Schofield said that the premises which were known as the Berney Arms had an on licence until 1902 and in those days the wherrymen used to call in for drinks. Now he wanted

to cater for the people on pleasure craft, the modern counterpart of the wherries. He already provided many facilities for pleasure craft.

Mr Laurence Vine (Messrs. Humphrey Lynde & Vine), who appeared for Mr Schofield, said there was no access by road. The nearest licenced premises were at Reedham and Yarmouth each five miles by river.

The application was supported by Mr. Alfred George Ward of Thorpe Old Hall, chairman of Norfolk and Suffolk Broads Yachtowners Association and by Mr. P. H. Liversidge, Commodore of Yarmouth and Gorleston Sailing Club who both said that they thought that the sale of liquor at the Old Inn would improve the facilities of that part of the river for people on pleasure craft.

Henry Hewitt, farmer and marshman, at Ash Tree Farm, said he had seen men employed by him on the marshes drink water out of a dyke because they were so thirsty.'

Figure 82. Mr Charlie Schofield in the Inn in the mid-1950's. (Pyett)

E.D.P. 1960
'FIRST FULL LICENCE SINCE 1902 TRAGEDY ON BROADS

THE OLD INN, Berney Arms, the isolated former wherry men's inn on the edge of Breydon Water, was granted a full licence by Blofield licensing justices yesterday.

Berney Arms Remembered

Supt. G. W. Bartram said he understood from the owner that the inn last had a full licence in 1902, but it had been withdrawn after a party from Burgh Castle had got drunk and three had been drowned on the return journey.

The owner, Mr Charles Leslie Schofield, told the justices that he had run a registered club at the inn since 1954 and also had an off-licence shop on the premises.

The inn, he said could be approached in good weather by a three-mile track from Wickhampton. It was half a mile from Berney Arms Halt, which left the main approach by the river. During the 1959 season 2000 boats had paid for moorings in front of the inn, said Mr. Schofield.

Club Members

In addition, 3000 boats had moored for periods of less than 15 minutes, while another 2000 had moored within reach of the inn.

Mr. Schofield said that at least one-third of his club members were also members of the Yarmouth and Gorleston Sailing Club, which had its headquarters at Burgh Castle. The remainder were locals, Norwich or Yarmouth residents and a "hard core" of regular visitors to the Broads.

The application was opposed by Charles James Farrant, of 18, Wellington Road, Yarmouth, who said he had looked after the Berney Arms Mill for the Ministry of Works for the last four and a half years.

His view was that if a full licence was granted more vessels would moor at the inn. It was already a dangerous place to moor and the increased traffic would increase the danger.

No Police Opposition

Supt. Bartram, said that although the police were not opposing the application it would not be possible to supervise the house in the normal way.

Mr. W. O. Carter (Hill & Perks). for Mr Schofield, said there had been no complaint about the running of the club or the mooring facilities. The only reason for Mr. Farrant's objection was that he did not like Mr Schofield.

The application was granted subject to confirmation, on the condition that the licence should run between March 15th and October 15th and that drinks should be served in the dining room only with meals.'

Some Past Occupants of the Berney Arms Public House:

Date	Name	Description / Notes	Reference
1836	John Cater	Victualler	Whites Directory
c.1840	William George	'Occupier', but did not live here.	Reedham Tithe Apportionment
1841	Robert Rushmer	Victualler	Reedham Census
1845	Robert Rushmer	Victualler	Whites Directory
1851	Horace Gillbert	Innkeeper	Reedham Census
1861	James Knights	Innkeeper	Reedham Census
1864	Charles Knights	Victualler / a brother to James and did not live on premises.	Whites Directory
1868	Charles Knights	Victualler	Harrods Directory
1871	James Knights	Innkeeper	Reedham Census

Berney Arms Remembered

Date	Name	Description / Notes	Reference
not given	Mr Carver	Innkeeper	'Black-Sailed Traders'
1881	Walter Daniels	Victualler / Farmer	Reedham Census
1883	Walter Daniels	Victualler	Whites directory
1886-1890	Frederick Carter	Victualler	Licence register
1891	Robert Thaxter	Publican	Reedham Census
1900	John Andrew	Victualler	Kellys Directory
1901	John Andrew	Victualler	Reedham Census
1904	John Andrew	Victualler	Kellys Directory
1908	John Andrew	Victualler	Kellys Directory
1909	John Andrew	Pub lost licence. Licence set to expire on 7 June 1910.	Ernest Hewitt Licence Register
1910	Thomas & Eliza Hewitt & family	He was Railway Platelayer, Blacksmith / Farmer. They used old inn as a farmhouse.	Ernest Hewitt
c.1933	Mr Cafferoy (?) & family	Kept goats inside.	Jack Carter
c.1937 to c.1942	Fred & Lilly Hewitt & family	Fred worked Breydon Pump	Ivan Mace
c.1943	Vacant	Roof needing repair.	Ivan Mace
c.1947	Aubrey Appleton & Dennis Robertson	Aubrey was a Musician. Bought the old inn from the Berney family. Removed floorboards and doors.	Ron Carter / Bob Mace
c.1949	Reginald & Elsie Matthews & family (Marguerite and June)	He renovated the buildings in 1950 and turned it into a guesthouse.	Reg Matthews / Peppy Matthews
c.1952	Dick & Muriel Foster		Joseph Williams
1953	Dick Forster	Club Licence obtained	Ron Carter
1954 to 1960	Charles L. Schofield & wife Gwen & family	He worked in an Electrical store in Yarmouth. Pub Off Licence was renewed in Feb. 1955 and full licence in 1960.	Joseph Williams. Gt. Yarmouth Mercury
c.1960 to 1964	Ken Barnes & family	Publican	Shelia Hutchinson
1964 to 1974	Bob Manning	Publican	Bob Manning
1974		Briefly owned by Northampton Brewery	Ivan Mace
c.1974 to 2000	Robert McLaughlan Steve	Publican	Sheila Hutchinson
2000 - present	Chris & Carole Harvey & family.	Tenants. Pub owned by Tapestry Taverns.	Sheila Hutchinson

Figure 83. The derelict Berney Inn in 1949 when Matthews bought it.
Top: View from the riverside, bottom: view from the rear. (Matthews)

Figure 84. Top: Side view of the pub hidden behind the old cowsheds in 1949. Bottom: the pub after restoration in 1951. (Matthews)

Peppy Matthews Remembers.

It was cold and the mud was very deep in the ruts, I was really scared, the dyke was only three feet away. I stood on the car's running board holding on to the car door for grim life. Father was adjusting the chains on the car wheels and laying down more sacks and things to obtain some sort of grip in the mud. We were stuck once again. This was a narrow lane between two dykes connecting two paddocks and through which the bullocks were continually being moved. My baby sister was crying, the dog howling and mother screeching about us all drowning in the muddy dykes or sinking into the marsh never to be seen again.

Figure 85. Marguerite 'Peppy' Matthews photographed, with a visiting guest's dog, on the riverwall, near the old inn in 1951. (M. Matthews)

We were later told our car was the first to cross the marshes. It was a large grey 20 horsepower Vauxhall with sumptuous leather interior.

"A hostile flat land with very large cows" was the first impression of a little girl, "but why were there no trees?" Could things get worse? It was awful, the old Inn was a derelict ruin, it was cold, damp, filthy, doors missing and windows out, holes in the roof; Well half gone really! My first trip upstairs was like a military operation. I was told "Step where I step". The floorboards were about a third missing, with a gap on the landing. I could see the downstairs rooms through the joists. Some ceilings had fallen down and I could feel the draught from the holes in the roof. It was broad daylight so I looked in fascination and listened to all the planning. I thought it all really exciting. This was my only look upstairs and I had strict orders not to attempt going upstairs until the floors had been repaired.

It was exciting from then on. Mother had hysterics over the 'snakes' which lived in the paddock behind the house, woke up one morning to a very large adder in the conservatory, which did not yet have a door on; father decapitated it as I recall and to make sure threw it in the river using the spade to carry it. It was a whopper, as thick as a man's arm and three feet long. We may be Londoners but we knew grass snakes were harmless so these were left. What a contrast from the bluebell woods of Sussex. I remember honeybees on Mallows, sea-asters and marran grass, the smell of mud, and the call of the gulls, the marsh still has a special magic for me.

I often met Harry ('Yoiton') who always seemed to be on patrol on the marsh, he was a kindly man. I was a very shy little girl and couldn't understand his 'foreign' language but we communicated once I was told he was the nice man from Ash Tree Farm. But what was he doing? His pockets were bulging. Would I like to stroke his furry little animal? What, that wicked man was killing moles! – he seemed to think it was ok to do so. I was eventually persuaded and did so, he told me they would make some fine lady a fur coat and that's better than digging up father's lawn.

To get to the station was a hazardous business especially for a little girl to have to 'walk the plank' over a wide dyke. The plank was often wet and slippery and once over you had to get through a herd of bullocks, which until I was used to them terrified me. I was seen to run but Harry knew everything and could see all things going on. He taught me how to manage them, if you could call it that, and in the end they either trotted after me like dogs or ignored me, depending how they felt or how near to the dyke plank they were. There were several to negotiate before I reached the station where Violet Mace sometimes waved as I crossed the line.

Mrs Hitchcock nearly had kittens the first time she saw me cross the marshes alone.

We owned our own 'milkers' and I had a pony so I was no stranger to animals even at that tender age.

There was always a bitter wind blowing so in the winter of 1951/2 the snow along our drive to the marsh was in a six-foot high drift.

We lived those first months, while the house was being renovated, in the old bar (dining room), bathing in a tin bath with water from the water butt outside.

One day I watched father dismantle the brick arches of the cellar. We found a little china dog and he set this in a concrete base for me and some opaque blue glass beads in the mortar of the brick wall. This became the larder of the kitchen.

The house looked beautiful, every bedroom was a different colour, and there was a fully plumbed bathroom overlooking the front porch, rond and river Yare.

The view across to Burgh Castle was always interesting. Lots of the boats went that way down the Waveney. There were many boats in the holiday season with people to wave to and a few wherries still on the water. Some boats 'blew-up' on Breydon Water while we were living here, caused by gas laying in the hull and igniting. Father rescued one bedraggled youth one afternoon after a terrific bang. He was as right as rain after a bath, fresh clothes and food, just grateful to have been thrown into the mud and be alive.

Berney Arms Remembered

I remember going to visit him in Yarmouth afterwards at his ironmongers shop.

My bedroom was downstairs, the window near the water butt, so when I heard music outside I crept along the corridor and upstairs to sneak into one of the front rooms to see the Golden Galleon go by. It was all lit up with people laughing and the ladies in pretty dresses.

To the right of the house a sewage treatment system was built; filter house one, two and three, with the water coming out clear and going into a dyke on the Breydon Water side. I found the large black connecting pipes very handy to sit on or swing from until I got found out. There was no hope of a cesspit, which would require emptying by tanker lorry as there was no road for access. The boats sent their sewage into the river.

On the mill side a new garden was laid after moving all the rubble and grasses. People said nothing would grow as it was salty but it did and the plants survived. I fed the goldfish and staked out the tortoise every day. The tortoise and the springer spaniel survived the first winter out there with us all in one room.

Mother and I were together when we saw an old man coming from Breydon direction along the towpath towards the Inn. "What's he up to?" she said, "there are no boats in view". She rushed out front but he was nowhere to be seen, we circled the house and still we could not see him, there was no hiding place as it was flat and the willows at the paddock were some distance away and there would not have been time for him to get there. We recounted this to father and later to 'Yoiton'. He knew who it was – an apparition, or as mother and Harry claimed a ghost. I found this very unnerving and took the dog about with me for several weeks after that, between babysitting.

It was while babysitting that I got clever, as one does at that age, playing 'beboos" when I fell 3 feet and slipped a disc in my neck. On my parents return they found I could not turn my head from side to side. What a frightening experience. That resulted in a trip in the River Inspector's boat across Breydon to Yarmouth where an ambulance met us. I spent the night in hospital and in the mid morning I snapped my head sideways and righted myself, thank goodness for that, there was talk of an operation. That afternoon father took me to a fish and chip shop restaurant near the market place and we had a meal out, a real treat, he was so nice I thought I dare not tell anyone now that I was larking about.

We went home by train the usual mode of transport, I think mother met us at the station in the pony and trap which was used for collecting guests and their luggage from the station.

I recall having tea with Mrs Hewitt of home made fare in her front room, father was outside with Harry and the little girls from 1 cottage were in the back room playing. They were very shy of mother and me. I held tightly onto my now toddling little sister always aware of the danger of the river and the dykes. Later Mrs Hewitt showed us around her home. I now know that the young girl was Sheila.

Father was the first private individual to commission the wherry Albion for years. It delivered all the furniture, outside equipment, and building materials, new roofing etc. When the furniture came the men dropped the real Turkish carpet in the river. Father caught the men as they were about to let it sink out of view because it was so large and very heavy. They didn't understand why he was so upset. Between them they managed to get it onto the bank, when it eventually dried out it was sent to be expertly dry-cleaned. The large sum of money needed, was recovered from the travel insurance cover. The carpet was eventually given to me as a wedding present, without the large border as the moths had eaten much of that, years before reducing its size.

When we left Berney father bought Overa House Farm and began breeding his own steers.

Figure 86. 'Elizabeth Simpson' was a volunteer lifeboat and also ran passenger sea-trips. Later she was converted and a wheelhouse added in 1980. When owned by Pleasure Steamers Ltd she ran trips to Berney Arms and Burgh Castle. Here she is moored at the Berney inn. (Allard)

Figure 87. The pub in 2000. (Hutchinson)

Figure 88. Top: Andy Mace, a descendent of Thomas & Eliza Hewitt who once lived here, serving behind the bar in 2001. Bottom: A view of the pub in 2002 showing the septic tank in the foreground to the left and new patio area to the right. (Hutchinson)

Figure 89. David Hewitt with his mother Lily at the Berney Arms reunion in September 2002. This was Lily's first trip back, for over 60 years, to the place where she, and husband Fred and family, once lived. (Hutchinson)

Figure 90. A group of people arriving at the pub in the boat 'Mandy Ann', having come from Burgh Castle for the 2002 reunion. (Barton)

Berney Arms Remembered

Mike Pickard Remembers

It was in the late 1950's that a friend and myself took to visiting the marshes to go sketching, initially around Mautby and Runham, then later going further a field to Reedham and Berney Arms on our cycles carrying our sketching gear.

My friend had the use of a Morris 1000 vehicle on one occasion in the mid-1960's and three of us set off for Wickhampton. Parking the car by the church, the day being fine and the sky reliable we set off on foot carrying our gear heading for Berney Arms. Being familiar with the liggers across the dykes we were able to cut across the marshes cutting quite a bit off the journey; though we had to keep an eye out for cattle grazing on the marshes. Arriving at the Berney pub we found it was open and what could be more tempting after a long walk on a hot day than to 'try one'! This led to several more beers so that by 2:30pm we felt inspired enough to venture out and do some painting.

To each his own so we went in different directions according to whatever view appealed to the beholder. The old eel fishermen's houseboat, the Greylag, attracted me but to get closer I had to cross a fair old dyke. There was a ligger but it was more like a pole in shape and it either rolled or I slipped going across and next thing I knew I was up to my waist in the stinking mud of the dyke. Thank heavens my mates hadn't seen or heard me, so I scrambled back on the bank, and talk about stink! I took my shoes and socks off rinsed them and left the socks to dry in the sun and sneaked back to a little shop, which was next to the pub to see if I could buy some trousers and socks, but no joy. Nothing for it but to go back and get on with the painting! I achieved a quite effective watercolour, working swiftly with vigorous brushstrokes, and captured the essence of the old structure and its surroundings. When we all reconvened, strangely enough at 6pm, opening

Figure 91. Mike Pickard by the scoopwheel of Howard's Mill on the Fleet c.1960. (Pickard)

time, I felt quite satisfied with my efforts. They had a bit of a chuckle at my falling in which I could not disguise, but that was better than them witnessing it, and we adjourned to the bar for an hour or so. When we came out the sun was still high but we had a long walk ahead.

One of my friends had laboured at an oil painting and as this takes some time to dry he had to leave it uncovered. The walk back was pleasant enough with a few beers inside us but being a warm evening the gnats were out in force and by the time we reached the car at Wickhampton the friends oil painting resembled a very large sticky flypaper. He was not amused. My painting, mounted and framed is still on the wall of a riverside

Berney Arms Remembered

bungalow at Martham and when I do occasionally see it I am still pleased with it and remember that day with a smile.

Sid Ward Remembers.

Sid was a fireman in the Acle turn out area during 1950 –1975 and they had to provide fire cover for the Berney Arms. Fortunately they were never called out to Berney.

One way of getting to Berney was to take an appliance from Wickhampton opening 9 marsh gates and then crossing the railway line at the Berney station crossing gates.

Another appliance would go to the Reedham station to put a pump and equipment on the next train to Berney.

In later years they retained a boat that could take the equipment out day or night. The fire service had also thought of putting at Berney a light pump and equipment which could be used by the locals, but this never materialised.

Gerald Banham Remembers

I worked for the Gorleston Coaling Company in the 1960's and in the summer I, and two other lorry drivers, Tony Howes and Ronald Pitts, took three lorries, each holding four tons of coal and coke out to Berney Arms. The delivery was shared between the pub, then owned by Manning, and Stanley Hewitt at the farmhouse.

We made our way to Wickhampton Church then over a very muddy track to the Berney Halt, thirty-three gates had to be opened and closed along the way. Our only sign was to make sure that each post had a white marker ring going out and a red ring coming back. All the cattle and horses on the marsh came over to see what was going on.

Once we had unloaded back we came bearing gifts of tomatoes, mushrooms and eggs. Getting back was never easy, the lorries now empty bounced and rolled in the deep ruts and we nearly always had broken eggs and squashed tomatoes. On at least two occasions we were caught in a rainstorm and we had to leave the lorries out there at Berney and get back to Yarmouth by train and then wait for a dry day to return to pick up the lorries.

On one bad winter the Inn ran out of coal and we had to take some to Burgh Castle and then across the river in a boat and carry it over the riverbank to deliver.

I remember the Berney Inn having a party in the 1970's and lots of people going from Burgh Castle Marina by boat. On the return trip Alfie Symonds fell in the river and said he never felt the cold.

I would go along the Acle straight road in one of the lorries to deliver coal to Britannia farm. At one time on arriving, a man came out of one of the sheds and asked what I wanted. "You have a coal delivery", I say. The man looked at me then replied, "You look a strong man. Can you help me? I have a cow having trouble delivering a calf". I helped and the calf was sadly stillborn. Afterwards I went to wash my hands and face over the top of a water barrel. The man says "Can you use the tap at the bottom as that is our drinking water".

Berney Arms Remembered

Ray Walpole Remembers

My visits to Berney were limited to one during WWII and another in about 1950. I recollect seeing a spectacular display from my bedroom window in Reedham one night in about 1942. I think there had been a raid on Yarmouth and someone mentioned that bombs had fallen over Berney. I became determined to collect some souvenirs and took the train from Reedham to Berney Arms. I started searching the marshes for shrapnel. To my surprise, not only did I find intact fins of incendiary bombs but complete unexploded ones as well. I collected three or four as well as the fins and mine fragments and travelled back on the train to Reedham in great excitement. However, as I mounted the station steps to the Railway Tavern, I bumped into PC Gilham. He asked me to show him the contents of my shopping bag, whereupon he confiscated the bombs. I cycled home in anger to tell my mum that, 'Ole Gilham pinched my bombs and only left me with the fins'. The danger of my find apparently never occurred to me, or the family! Still I cleaned up the aluminium fins so that we could use them as flower vases.

BREYDON WATER AND HOUSEBOATS

Breydon Water is Britain's largest inland tidal water. It is about 4 miles long and one mile wide at its widest point. At low water vast mudflats appear on either side of the navigational channel. These flats are almost all mud brought down river by the Yare and the Waveney and deposited here. The level of the mudflats is fairly uniform except at the edges of the navigational channel where the mud is slightly higher and this causes the water to be retained on the mudflats at low tide and to flow away slowly through natural drains. The mud is usually visible at low tide for about an hour, and is covered by about 3 or 4 feet of water at high tide.

The mudflat is firm enough for walking if great care is taken but the edges of the drains can be soft. The Carters who had a houseboat near the Berney inn often went eel catching on Breydon, sometimes babbing and sometimes with a net. If fishing with a net, they would walk across the mudflats and select a drain. Two of them would hold the net across the mouth of the drain and the others would walk along the drain with a plunging pole driving eels and flounders towards the net.

The mudflats provide the food for many species of wildfowl and birds such as the Turnstone, Grey Heron, Oyster Catcher, Redshank and Ringed Plover etc., which feed on the grubs and insect living here. The bird life on and around Breydon Water has over the years attracted many wildfowlers, birdwatchers and naturalists. Arthur Patterson, the naturalist and author spent much time around Breydon and had a houseboat on Breydon. Robin Harrison the naturalist, who wrote for the Gt Yarmouth Mercury, and who became the first Breydon Warden also had a houseboat on Breydon. The RSPB now are the wardens for this nature reserve.

Figure 92. Top: Robin Harrison in his punt on Breydon Water circa 1940 (M. Browne). Bottom: Robin Harrison with P.W. (Billy) Browne and Peter Browne bird watching from Robin's houseboat 'Lapwing' in March 1940. (P. Browne)

Figure 93. Top: Jack, Ron and Bob Carter in front of the 'Greylag' houseboat on the rond near the Berney Inn in the 1950's. Bottom: Jack Carter stirring up eels and flounders in Breydon Water. (R. Carter)

Berney Arms Remembered

Ron Carter Remembers.

Ron and his relatives and friends had a houseboat 'Greylag' at Breydon not far from the Berney Inn.

One day Henry Hewitt 'Yoiton' was going to fetch the cows in for milking and he was riding his bike across the marshes with his dog running at his side. The cows were on the marsh past the Inn and all the gates were open. 'Yoiton' stopped to talk to Ron and his cousin John and sent the dog on to fetch the cows in. When the cows came in with the dog behind them John says to 'Yoiton', " How do you know the dog has brought all the cows in and not missed any?" Yoiton say, "The dog has done it enough times now it can count them".

Figure 94. The houseboat 'Pintail II' circa 1960 (Pickard). This houseboat was around until 1965.

Figure 95. Top: Peter Allard on 8th September 1963 in his 14 foot gunpunt at Berney Arms. Bottom: Peter Allard at his houseboat on the rond near the Breydon Dickey Works in 1964. (Allard)

Figure 96. The houseboat 'White Swan' owned by George Rose was on Duffel's Rond from 1964. Top: photographed 1st March 1969 with Lockgate Farm in the distance (Allard). Bottom: on 25th April 1990 with Lockgate mill in the distance. It was wrecked on 26th February 1990.

Figure 97. Top: the RSPB boat on Breydon Water on 26 August 2002 (Allard). Bottom: Donnie Hubbard and Roy Carr fishing 1 May 2000. (Allard)

Figure 98. Top: 'Resolute' on Breydon Water in the mid 1950's. She began broads trips along the Waveney in 1946 and was sold to the Veteran Steamship Society in 1967 (Pyett). Bottom: An RAF Puma helicopter carrying sandbags onto Breydon Wall on 11th January 1976. (Allard)

Berney Arms Remembered

DICKEY WORKS (TG475062)

At the far western end of Breydon Water is the 'Dickey Works'. This is the name given to the old tide jetty or breakwater, constructed for the purpose of deflecting the ebb tide into the deep channel across the estuary towards Yarmouth. Without this, the tide would sweep across the entire width of the estuary .It was near this 'Dickey Works' that Peter Allard had his houseboat moored on an adjacent salting in the early 1960's.

Research by Peter Allard in recent years, mainly through old maps and literature, has thrown some light on the origins of the Dickey Works. They have been mentioned as being built in about 1832 and the few available maps of this period suggest that this date is probably correct. James Walker's very detailed map of 1826 (when he was under contract to Great Yarmouth Port and Haven Commissioners) does not show this construction, but it clearly appears on Emerson's map of 1854, marked 'Tide Jetty. Booth's map of 1872 shows it clearly marked as the 'Dickey Works'

With the constant silting up of Breydon Water in the early half of the 19th century, the intransigent efforts of the Great Yarmouth Port and Haven Commissioners (the forebears of the present Great Yarmouth Port Authority) resulted in much pressure from users to maintain a navigable passage across the estuary.

James Walker, a consultant engineer, was employed in 1826 to advise on the practicability of making Breydon Water navigable for vessels drawing up to ten feet. In 1828 the Commissioners' brand new steam dredger began operating at Breydon and in its first full year of operation raised some 60,000 tons of mud at an average cost of £1 per 60 tons. The Commissioners' archives indicate that during this period, they were also operating a 'Horse Dydling Engine', the eight scoops of which were geared to a whim made to revolve by two horses. In 1828, this raised 14,325 tons of mud at an average cost similar to that of the steam dredger. The suspicions are that it was the 'Horse Dydling Engine' which was responsible for building the tide jetty (alias 'the 'Dickey Works'). The word 'Dickey' was the old local name for a horse or donkey. Some confirmation of this appears in Arthur Patterson's 'Nature in Eastern Norfolk' (1905) which states that the 'Dickey Works' were built by a contractor who had a small paddle-boat worked by a donkey -locally known as a 'dickey'! He continues —'hence the characteristic naming of the construction.'

Most likely was that the contractor (James Walker & Go.) hired the 'Horse Dydling Engine' and adapted this also for pile-driving, presumable quite an easy conversion. The 'Dickey Works' tide jetty was originally boarded up with planks of wood along its entire length. According to Harry 'Yoiton' Hewitt, these planks were regularly pilfered by the locals for a variety of uses.

The 'Yarmouth Mercury' states in 1932, that the 'Dickey Works' were in a ruinous state and this deterioration has certainly continued. Today the double row of stakes are badly weather beaten, totally rotten and certainly not boarded. At the extreme eastern end, a pile of flint stones can clearly be seen at very low tides and it is possible that the whole structure was at one time filled in with these. The ebb tide now flows completely through the derelict tide jetty, as it did prior to its construction in the 1830s.

Consequently, to some extent, the entire western end of Breydon Water has deepened within living memory.

There appears to be some confusion in various local Broadland literature over the actual site of the 'Dickey Works'. Several state, including Patterson in some of his later books in the 1930's that the 'Dickey Works' were at the confluence of the rivers Yare and Waveney. (TG471052) This additional tide jetty was constructed much later in 1864, using the Port & Haven Commissioners' steam dredger for dredging and an engine and bell for driving the piles. This tide jetty, also derelict, and the original 'Dickey Works' were both referred to by Patterson in the 1930s as 'Dickey Works'. It seems likely that the name 'Dickey Works' was verbally transferred to the much later tide jetty by Breydoners and Berneyites over the succeeding years.

BREYDON PUMP (TG477070)

The Havergate Fleet originally entered Breydon water by a sluice gate but a diesel pump

Figure 99. Construction gang working for T. Smithdale & Sons of Acle, building the diesel pump at Breydon in 1933. (Havis)

was built in 1933 and began to work in 1934. It was capable of pumping 35 tons of water per minute from the Fleet.

The diesel pump was replaced with an electric pump. Work began on the new electric pump in 1946 and the plant, consisting of two motors, was installed by Smithdale & Sons. The new pump was officially opened in October 1948 by Mr H Gardiner of the Ministry of Agriculture and Fisheries, and is capable of discharging up to 138,000 tons of water in 24 hours from the Fleet into Breydon Water. The old green diesel pumphouse still

Berney Arms Remembered

stands alongside the redbrick building holding the electric pump.

Fred Hewitt looked after the diesel pump when he lived at the old Berney Arms pub in the late 1930's and early 1940's. Reggie Mace operated the pump when he worked for Fred Hewitt. 'Yoiton' worked the electric pump after he moved into Ashtree Farm at Berney Arms and he continued to work the electric pump for a couple of years after he moved to Cobholm. Stanley Hewitt then took over from 'Yoiton' and worked the pump for a couple of years until the Drainage Board put their own man in charge. The electric pump is now automatic with sensors to detect the water levels and turn the pump on and off accordingly.

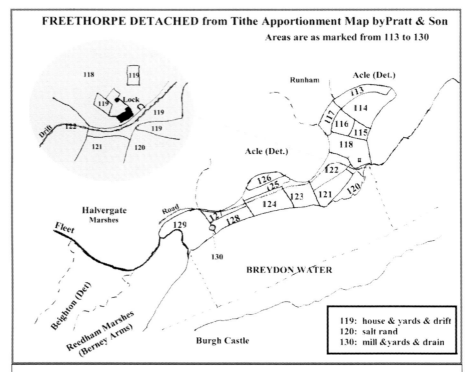

FREETHORPE DETACHED from Tithe Apportionment Map byPratt & Son

Areas are as marked from 113 to 130

119: house & yards & drift
120: salt rand
130: mill & yards & drain

Figure 100. From the Freethorpe Tithe Apportionment map we find that the whole of the detached portion of the Parish, areas 113 to 130, is occupied by Henry Gowing and owned by Robert Cory, the younger, and Philip Blundell Nesbitt. Area 119 is labelled as 'House Yards and drift' and was the site of Lockgate Farm, while Area 130 is labelled as 'Mill, Yards and Drain' and is the site of the Lockgate Mill and marsh house. No marsh-house is mentioned here by the mill, however, suggesting it was built later. (Note: These marshes were sold by Nesbitt in Sept 1877 by Auction to a Mr William Butcher. The selling Agent was Samuel Aldred.)

122

Berney Arms Remembered
LOCKGATE MILL AND MARSH HOUSE (TG480072)

Located in Freethorpe Detached Parish, Lockgate mill also known as **Freethorpe Mill, Banham's Black Mill and Duffel's Mill**. Although located close to the Breydon Pump, it is not on the Halvergate Fleet but drains its own marshes. It was not marked on Faden's map of 1797 but was marked on Bryant's map of 1826 as Freethorpe Mill.

The mill is four storeys high, built in red brick and tarred black. The brickwork stands 35 feet high and it is about 24 feet overall diameter at the base and had four windows and two doors. It carried four patent sails, which turned clockwise and drove a large external scoop wheel, 19 feet in diameter with seven-inch wide paddles.

When it was put up for sale in 1877 it was described as 'recently erected by Smithdales of Acle' so the existing mill was probably a rebuild. A small steam engine may have been installed either here or by the Breydon pump in the early 1900's for a time, as Arthur Patterson mentioned such an engine in his book of 1907 and said Dan Banham was the marshman.

Bob Banham operated the mill around 1912 and Gordon Addison, who lived at nearby Lockgate Farm, is believed to have looked after the mill for a time in the 1920's. The mill was last worked in the mid-1940's by Leonard Carter. The mill then remained derelict and the sails were blown down in 1953. A temporary aluminium cap was fitted in 1985, and in November 1988 the mill with the stocks lying on the floor, and the derelict marsh house, then owned by the Banham family, went up for sale by auction with an expected price of £8,000 to £12,000 and was bought by Mr Kim Baker for £16,000. The mill is still owned by Mr Baker, and remains derelict. Amongst the previous owners was Sir Humphrey de Trafford.

There was a fire at the mill in April 2001, probably caused by vandals. Because of the foot and mouth restrictions imposed at the time the fire engine sent to the fire had to wait on the concrete road for someone to come along to disinfect it, before it could go across the marsh track to the mill.

The **Marsh House**, which stood next to the mill had a tiled roof and was built of Suffolk whites bricks, and was tarred black the same as the mill. The house had two bedrooms upstairs and two living rooms downstairs. The kitchen was built separate and you had to go outside to get to it. It also had a dairy. There was no electricity and cooking was done with a coal-fired cooking range. Water was obtained from the roof and collected in tanks. The Tithe Map of about 1840 does not mention a marsh house here and so it must have been built sometime later.

Jack French, who worked for the Banham family, lived here with his family for a few years before 1952 and again after the 1953 floods for a while (they lived in the cottages at Berney Arms in 1952-3) The damaged sails of the mill were laying beside the mill and they used them for firewood. Lenny Rose occupied the marsh house for a short period before the French family.

Len Carter was here from 1931 till about 1945 and was last marshman to work the mill. Jimmy Banham lived here before Len Carter according to Ernest Hewitt, a cousin to Jimmy Banham, and in the 1937 Kelly's directory a Mr James Banham is listed as marshman for Freethorpe, but Len Carter was in residence at that time.

Figure 101. Top: Lockgate Mill in working order in 1936 with marsh house on the left (Perry). Bottom: P.W. Browne and his sons Mike and Pat eating sandwiches, sitting on straw pile outside Lockgate Mill, whose sails, one of which is seen here, are down, in the winter of 1946/47. (M. Browne)

Figure 102. Lockgate Mill deterioration. Top: 1950's (M. Horton), bottom left: circa 1960 (Pickard), right: circa 1980's. (M. Horton)

Berney Arms Remembered

In 1936, the author and naturalist, Richard Perry stayed with the Carter family at the marsh house for a time while he wrote his book 'At The Turn Of The Tide'. Dorothy Hanton, nee Carter remembers that Peter Scott was also intending to come and stay with them for a while but WWII broke out and so he never made the visit.

LOCKGATE FARM (TG494077)

This large farmhouse was marked on Faden's map of 1797 and on all subsequent maps. It has generally been known as Lockgate Farm or Lockgate House but has also been referred to as 'Duffell's House'. The older part of the building was constructed of small two inch bricks with wrought iron window frames, suggesting it was very old. The rest of the house was built later with the larger two and a half inch bricks. It was a large house with a total of eleven rooms, six of them bedrooms upstairs, and two of them large parlours downstairs. Access to one of the rooms upstairs was only by its own staircase from the dairy.

The house and outbuildings stood till 1981 when everything was demolished. It had stood empty for several years prior to this falling into disrepair and suffering from the effects of vandals.

The original purpose of the building is uncertain. It has been suggested that it was a tollhouse as it was situated on the old drift-way track going from Yarmouth to Halvergate and Wickhampton. The Tithe map has a 'lock' marked by the house but we can only guess at what kind of lock this was. As the course of the Halvergate Fleet and other natural creeks may have changed in the far distant past is it possible that one once entered Breydon near this house and sluicegates or lockgates were once located here?

The last occupants at the house were Gordon and Mary Ann Addison who lived here from the early 1920's. Gordon was not a local man but his wife was a daughter of Daniel Key and Jane Banham who were local marsh folk. She died in 1960 and Gordon died, still living here on the marshes, in 1967. They had no electric or water at the house and relied on paraffin lamps, coal-fires and rainwater. Their post was delivered to a box about half a mile away next to the railway line, and coal was delivered only once a year when the marshes were dry enough to get a truck across the marshes.

Gordon was a marshman who looked after cattle and horses for Deny Wright and others. Often he would have more than a thousand cattle to tend. He is believed to have worked the Lockgate drainage mill for a time in the 1920's and, like the other marshmen, also did thistle-topping and dyke-drawing. The Addisons kept their own pigs, cows, chicken, geese, ducks, horse and dogs. Mary Ann made butter and cheese and they had a stall on Yarmouth market where they sold their produce.

Gordon had a bike and cycled to Yarmouth along the Breydon wall every week to collect provisions and if Mary Ann wanted to go to the town she would go across the marshes to the Acle New Road going by horse and trap. There was about seventeen gates to go through on the trip across the marshes.

Figure 103. Top: Lockgate Farm House, bottom: Gordon Addison. (Allard)

Figure 104. Top: Lockgate Farm house with Phylis and Nevile Browne and Reg Cable on the river wall (M. Horton). Bottom: Lockgate Farm house circa 1960. (M. Pickard)

Berney Arms Remembered

THE BERNEY FAMILY.

The Berney family is said to have come from Normandy before the Norman Conquest and to have settled at 'Berney' near Walsingham. When they first came to Reedham is not certain but a Thomas de Berney married a Margaret de Redham in about 1360.

Margaret was the sole surviving heir of the de Redham family, being a descendant of Richard de Redham who was the Lord of the Manor in Reedham at the time of the Doomsday book in 1086.

The Berney family have been associated with Reedham ever since and became major landowners in Reedham, and across the whole of Norfolk. The Berney Arms hamlet, which is part of the Reedham Parish is named after the Berney family and was built on land belonging to the Berney family.

Although most of the land at Berney Arms has been sold off in recent times, much of it in 1986 to the RSPB, some marshes to the north of the railway line are still owned by Mr John Verel Berney.

His family tree can be traced back to Henry and Alice Berney who are commemorated on the Berney alter in Reedham Church, and further back to Thomas de Berney mentioned above.

Ancestry for John Verel BERNEY:

1. **John Verel BERNEY** was born 1924, the eldest son of
   George Augustus BERNEY, born 1865, died Oct 1952, and Marjory Scott **VEREL**.
   (Note J.V. Berney sold Morton Hall in 1963.)
2. **George Augustus BERNEY** was the son of
   Augustus BERNEY, born 1831, died 1910 and Matilda **GIBBS**.
   (Note G.A. Berney was Lord of the Manor of Bracon Ash.)
3. **Augustus BERNEY** was the fourth son of
   Thomas Trench BERNEY, born 27 Jul 1784, died 1869 and Mary **PENRICE**.
   (Note: the eldest son of Thomas Trench was **George Duckett Berney**, who married Katherine Mary **Lombe**, but who died in 1887 without a son and heir).
4. **Thomas Trench BERNEY** was the only son of
   Thomas BERNEY, born 18 Mar 1753, died 21 Nov 1786, and Elizabeth **JACKSON**.
   (Note: T.T. Berney bought Morton Hall in 1819. He was sheriff of Norfolk in 1813.)
5. **Thomas BERNEY** was the only son of
   John BERNEY, born 14 Jul 1717, died c.1800, and Susan **TRENCH**.
6. **John BERNEY** was a son of
   Thomas BERNEY, born c.1674, died 1720 and Anne **SUCKLING**.
   (Note: J. Berney bought Bracon Hall, Bracon Ash in about 1750.)
7. **Thomas BERNEY** was the son of
   John BERNEY, born 1634, died 1678, and Elizabeth **ONSLOW**.
8. **John BERNEY** was eldest son of
   Thomas BERNEY, born c.1599, died c. 1673 and Dorothy **SMITH**.

9. **Thomas BERNEY** was son of
   Thomas BERNEY, born c.1548, died c.1616 and Juliana **GAWDY**.
   (Notes: T. Berney bought Gowthorpe Manor, Swardston in 1630. His brother Richard was created the first baronet of Parkhill, Reedham.in 1620.)
10. **Thomas BERNEY** was eldest son of
    Henry BERNEY, born c.1525, died c.1584 and Alice **APPLETON**.
11. **Henry BERNEY** was son of
    John BERNEY, born c. 1500 and Margaret **READ**.
12. **John BERNEY** was a son of
    John BERNEY, born c.1455 and Margaret **WENTWORTH**.
13. **John BERNEY** was a son of
    John BERNEY, born c.1423 and Elizabeth **MONDEFORD**.
14. **John BERNEY** Was a son of
    Thomas BERNEY, born c.1388.
15. **Thomas BERNEY** Was a son of
    John BERNEY, born c.1362, and Isabel **HEVINGHAM**
16. **John BERNEY** was a son of
    Thomas BERNEY, born c1336 and Margaret **De REDHAM**.

BERNEY ARMS CENSUS RECORDS
Berney Arms is in the parish of Reedham and the available censuses have been examined. Unfortunately specific addresses were not given and apart from the 1901, 1891 and 1881 censuses, which are relatively straight forward, I have had to deduce which were the people living at Berney Arms. Additional notes from other sources are placed in ( ) brackets.

1901 Census (RG13/1855)
186: Seven Mile House

Robert Burgess	41	Dairy Farmer (son of George)
Elizabeth Burgess	32	Wife
Robert Burgess	7	Son
Alice Burgess	14	Sister
Harry Bedingfield	17	Farm Servant

Farmhouse Uninhabited (This is the marsh house near 7-mile where Thaxter family lived)
187: Cottage 1:

James Farrow	60	Widower/marshman/cattle stockman
William Farrow	23	Marsh labourer
John Farrow	26	Marsh labourer (dies 1949, middle name Alfred, nickname 'Jack'.)

Florence Farrow	23	Dau-in-law/Dom housekeeper (wife to John, middle name Mary, dies Sept 1968)

188: Cottage 2:

James Farrow	28	Marsh labourer (son of above James Farrow?)
Sarah A. Farrow	27	Wife from Burgh Castle
George R. Hewitt	6	Stepson
James W. Farrow	2	from Burgh Castle

189: Cottage 3

Edward Banham	23	Marshman from Wickhampton (son of Bob Banham of the Butterfly Mill on the Halvergate Fleet)
Mary Ann Banham	23	Wife from Chedgrave (nee Hewitt dau of King Billy)
Frances Banham	3	Daughter
Grace Banham	1	Daughter

190: Cottage4

William Patrick	32	Widower/Marsh lab (nickname 'Tooshe', later at Haddiscoe Dam)
Stephen Patrick	12	Son
Blanche Patrick	9	Daughter (attended Berney Arms school and then Reedham school from 14-4-1902)
William Patrick	7	Son (later marshman by New Cut in Raveningham Detached Parish)
Ernest Patrick	6	Son
Pamela Patrick	22	Sister/housekeeper. From Morley St Botolph

191: Ashtree Farm

William Hewitt	61	Dairy farmer (dies 1928, nicknamed King Billy)
Susanna Hewitt	63	Wife from Gt Yarmouth (his 2nd wife, she dies 1914)
James Hewitt	19	Son (middle name David, nickname 'Westmacot', later becomes the marshman at Ravenhall on the Island, and then here at Berney in 1924, dies Jan. 1968)
Eunice Hurrell	25	Stepdaughter, from Gt Yarmouth

192: Bungalow

Isaac Hewitt	36	Millwright (son of King Billy, dies Dec 1946)
Emma Hewitt	46	Wife from Fritton (dies Dec 1932)
George Hewitt	14	Son (later railway carpenter and millwright, dies Dec 1980)
Fred Hewitt	13	Son
William Hewitt	11	Son
Daisy Hewitt	9	Daughter
Blanche Bruce	19	Stepdaughter/domestic

193: Cottage 6/7

Charles Beddingfield	43	Gen. Labourer
Jane Beddingfield	44	Wife

Albert Beddingfield	11	Son
Lilly Beddingfield	9	Daughter
Harriet Beddingfield	7	Daughter
Arthur Beddingfield	5	Son
Annie Beddingfield	3	Daughter

194: The Inn

John Andrews	45	Licensed victualler
Sarah Andrews	40	Wife
Robert Andrews	21	Gen lab
William Andrews	18	Son
Arthur Andrews	16	Son
Fredrick Andrews	15	Son
Ethel Andrews	13	Daughter
Lilly Andrews	11	Daughter
Elizabeth Andrews	9	Daughter
Ada Andrews	6	Daughter

(attended Berney Arms school)

Dora Andrews	3	Daughter

(attended Berney Arms school)

195: The Station

Thomas Johnson	57	Signalman
Elizabeth Johnson	56	Wife

196: The Station

Thomas Hewitt   38   Platelayer
(son of King Billy, dies 1927)

Eliza Hewitt   33   Wife
(nee Banham, middle name Francis, dies Feb 1953)

Robert Hewitt   12
(middle names Last Benjamin, dies Feb 1940)

Henry Hewitt   10
(nickname 'Yoiton', middle name Bumbury, later marshman at Ravenhall then at Berney Arms Ash Tree Farm, dies June 1974))

Harriet Hewitt   7
(middle name Ann, dies Sept 1975, marries her cousin William George Benjamin Hewitt. He attended Berney Arms school then Reedham from 21-4-1902)

Rose Hewitt   5
(middle name Emma, marries 1st Sid Gibbs, 2nd Mr Martin)

Funeral Of Mrs. E. F. Hewitt.—The funeral of Mrs. Eliza Frances Hewitt, widow of Mr. Thomas Hewitt, of Station Cottage, Berney Arms, took place at Reedham Church. Mrs. Hewitt, who was 84, died at her son's home. Coming to live on the marshes at an early age, Mrs. Hewitt spent all her married life at Berney Arms. She had 13 children, eight of whom survive her. Immediate mourners were Mrs. G. Small, Mrs. R. Martin, Mrs. W. Hewitt, Mr. H. Hewitt, Mr. and Mrs. E. Hewitt, Mr. R. Mace, Mr. and Mrs. D. Gibson, Miss J. Mace, Miss B. Mace, Mr. Russell Mace, Mr. S. Hewitt, Mr. T. Hewitt, Mr. Robert Mace, Mr. B. Hewitt, Mr. I. Mace, Mr. S. Gibbs, Mr. H. Gibbs, Miss D. Hewitt, Mrs. J Hewitt, Mr. I. Hewitt, Mr. A. Hewitt, Mr. W. Hewitt, Mr. G. Hewitt, Mr. and Mrs. W. Farrow, Nurse Jackson, Mr. F. Burgess, Mrs. G. Tibbenham and Mrs. Brinded.

Figure 105. Studio portrait of Eliza Hewitt.

Berney Arms Remembered

| James Hewitt | 3 | (middle name David, drowned off HM Drifter Fennew May 1917) |
| Thomas Hewitt | 3mths | (middle name Fred, born 26-12-1900)) |

1891 Census: (April 5-6th.) Ref RG12/1539.

187: Nr Reedham (marsh house near 7-mile House)

| James Thaxter | 63 | Marshman |
| Sophie Thaxter | 57 | Wife |

186: Seven Mile House:

George Burgess	61	Marsh Farmer
Harriet Burgess	49	Wife (previously Harriet Bullman)
Henry Burgess	20	Gen. Lab.
Alice Burgess	4	
Matilda Clarke	18	Dom. Serv.

185: Cottage 1:

Frederick Carter	43	Gen. Lab.
Louise Carter	39	Wife
Leonard Carter	12	
Hilda E. Carter	10	
Frederick Carter	7	

184: Cottage 2:

James Farrow	50	Gen. Lab.
Mary A. Farrow	43	Wife
James Farrow	21	Fisherman
William Farrow	12	Son
May Farrow	7	

183: Cottage 3:

| Robert Burgess | 30 | Marsh Farmer (came from 7-Mile Hs and returns there as marshman) |
| Elizabeth Burgess | 23 | Wife |

182: Cottage 4:

William A.Patrick	24	Gen. Lab.
Jane Patrick	34	Wife (nee Hewitt, dau of King Billy)
Herbert A.Patrick	3	
Stephen Patrick	2	
Blanche Patrick	3 days	
Frances Patrick	25	Sister

181: Ashtree FarmHouse:

William Hewitt	50	Marshman (King Billy)
Harriet Hewitt	49	Wife (nee Pettingill, dies June1898)
Robert F. Hewitt	22	Lab.
George Hewitt	18	Lab. (later marshman at Ravenhall on the Island)
Henry A. Hewitt	15	Lab.

Mary A. Hewitt	12	Daughter (later marries Ted Banham)
James D. Hewitt	8	Son (nickname 'Westmacott')
Harriet F. Legget	24	Gen. Serv.

180: Bungalow:

Isaac J. Hewitt	25	Journeyman Millwright
Rose E. Hewitt	35	Wife
George E. Hewitt	3	Son (born 7-2-1887, dies Dec 1980)
Frederick A.Hewitt	2	Son (middle name Arnold, born 30-3-1888)
William R. Hewitt	1	Son (born 26-7-1889
Gertrude Bruce	9	Stepdaughter (marries Billy Farrow)
Evelyn Bruce	8	Stepdaughter
Lucy Perry	15	Servant

179: Cottage 6:

George Burgess	38	Fisherman
Elizabeth Burgess	37	Wife
Sarah Burgess	17	
Caroline Burgess	15	
James Burges	14	
George Burgess	12	
Mary Burgess	8	
William Burgess	6	
Benjamin Burgess	4	
Daniel Burgess	2	
Frederick Burgess	5mths.	

178: Cottage 7:

Charles Bedingfield	34	Gen. Lab.
Jane Bedingfield	35	Wife
George Bedingfield	10	
Harry Bedingfield	7	(living & working at 7mile house in 1901)

Figure 106, Thomas Hewitt

Charles Bedingfield	5	(middle name Edward, in hospital in 1901, marries Beatrice Emily Burrage, dies 1932)
Beatrice Bedingfield	3	
Albert Bedingfield	3	
Lilly Bedingfield	1	

177: Berney Arms Inn:

Robert Thaxter	53	Publican (in 1861 a marshman in cottages, in 1851 at 7 mile House)
Elizabeth Thaxter	55	Wife
Florence Fish?	20	Daughter

176: Station Cottage 1:

Thomas Hewitt	29	Railway Platelayer
Eliza Hewitt	22	Wife (nee Banham)

| William Banham | 7 | Son (William Thomas James Banham, born out of wedlock, dies Oct 1923) |
| Robert Hewitt | 2 | Son (dies Feb 1940) |

175: Station Cottage 2:

William Edwards	61	Railway Platelayer
Harriet Edwards	62	Wife
Thomas Edwards	27	Railway Signalman
Eliza Edwards	21	
Sidney Edwards	4	Grandchild
Harriet Edwards	2	Grandchild
Maude Edwards	2 mths.	Grandchild

1881 Census: (April 3-4th) Ref RG11/1946.

Only ten entries at Berney Arms itself so one dwelling must be unoccupied!

180: (marsh house near 7-mile)

| James Thaxter | 53 | Marshman |

181: Seven Mile House:

George Burgess	52	Marshman
Robert Burgess	20	Marshman (living at Cottages at Berney in 1891 and returns here by 1901)
Elizabeth Burgess	17	
Abraham Burgess	13	
Henry Burgess	10	
Harriet Bullman	39	Housekeeper (later marries George Burgess)

182: cottage (1?):

George Chapman	23	Marsh Lab.
Harriet Chapman	28	Wife
George Chapman	1	

183: cottage (2?):

James Farrow	40	Lab. Cement Works
Mary Ann Farrow	34	Wife
Harriet Farrow	13	
James Farrow	11	
John Farrow	8	
William Farrow	3	

184: cottage (3?):

George Thaxter	39	Waterman (possibly a son of John Thaxter?)
Harriet Thaxter	68	Mother
Mary Ann Farrow	17	Dom. Servant (later marries Stephen Hewitt on the Island, dies 1918)

185: Farmhouse:

| John Burgess | 52 | Marshman (at Railway cottages nr. 7-mile in 1891) |
| Harriet Burgess | 48 | Wife (at Railway cottages nr. 7-mile in 1891) |

Jane Hubbard	27	Daughter
Robert Hubbard	28	Journeyman Carpenter
Ernest A. Hubbard	6	G'son (at Railway cottages nr. 7-mile in 1891)
Albert R. Hubbard	5	G'son

186: Bungalow:

Frederick Carter	32	Gen. Lab. (licensee at Berney Arms pub circa 1886 to 1890)
Louise Carter	28	Wife
Edith Carter	5	
Leonard Carter	2	

187: cottage (6?):

William Thaxter	30	Marshman
Louisa Thaxter	30	Wife
William Thaxter	13	Gen. Lab.
Rosa Thaxter	10	
Almira Thaxter	8	
Percy Thaxter	7	
Herbert Thaxter	6	
Kate Thaxter	3	
Alberta Thaxter	6mths	

188: cottage (7?):

Charles Beddingfield	22	Waterman
Jane Beddingfield	23	Wife
George H.Beddingfield	2mths	

189: Berney Arms Inn:

Walter Daniels	24	Licensed Vict / Farmer 25 acres
Ellen Daniels	22	Wife
George Daniels	2	
Archibald Daniels	4mths	
James Blake	56	Cabinet maker – boarder

190: station cottage:

William Edwards	52	Platelayer
Harriet Edwards	53	Wife
Mary A. Edwards	14	
Eliza Edwards	11	
Charlotte Edwards	9	

191: station cottage:

George Peart	63	Platelayer
Sarah Peart	65	Wife

1871 Census: (April 2-3rd) Ref RG10/1829.
29: By the River (marsh house near 7-mile)

James Thaxter	43	Marshman

Maria Thaxter	77	Mother?
Maria Thaxter	43	Sister
Walter Thaxter	14	Nephew (middle name Joseph dies 1953, Bur Reedham)

30: Seven Mile House:

George Burgess	43	Marshman (son of James and was at Wickhampton in 1861)
Elizabeth Burgess	44	Wife
Benjamin Burgess	23	Marshman
Harriet Burgess	20	
George Burgess	13	
James Burgess	11	
Robert Burgess	9	
Elizabeth Burgess	6	
Abraham Burgess	3	
Henry Burgess	11mths	
Mary A. Mallet	19	Servant / dairymaid
John Page	70	visitor / labourer

31: By the River (1?):

Mary Carver	71	Cowkeeper
John Baker	45	Lodger / Chelsea pensioner
William Lanham		Lodger / lab.
Thomas Milligan		Lodger / lab.

32: By the River (2?):

John Thaxter	57	Marshman (probably a son of Joseph Thaxter?)
Harriet Thaxter	55	Wife
Harriet Thaxter	22	Daughter

33: By the River (3?):

John Stubbs	55	Lab.
Elizabeth Stubbs	53	Wife
Louisa Stubbs	15	
Ellen Stubbs	13	
Sarah Stubbs	11	

34: By the River (4?):

James Farrow	29	Lab.
Mary Ann Farrow	24	Wife
Mary Ann Farrow	7	(marries Stephen Hewitt)
Harriet Farrow	3	
James Farrow	1	

35: Farmhouse (Ashtree?)

John Burgess	42	Marsh Farmer 63 acres
Harriet Burgess	37	Wife
Jane Burgess	17	(later marries Robert Hubbard)

Millicent Hanton	3	Niece
Eliza Culley	28	Charwoman
James Etheridge	18	Servant/lab.

36: By the river (bungalow?):

Robert Bull	49	Cement maker / clay labourer
Maria Bull	43	Wife
Charles Bull	17	Lab.
Maria Bull	14	
George Bull	11	
Harriet Bull	8	
Eliza Bull	6	
Emily Bull	4	
Edward Bull	2	
Eliza Bacon	52	Boarder

37: By the River (6?):

James Knights	22	Lab.
Caroline Knights	21	Wife
George Knights	1	

38: By the River (7?):

John Green	29	Lab.
Frances Green	30	Wife
Frederick Green	4	

39: Berney Arms Inn:

James Knights	44	Innkeeper (died 1876?)
Maria Knights	44	Wife
Henry Knights	16	Lab.
Johnathon Knights	13	(later becomes a wherryman)
Martha? Knights	8	
Eliza Knights	6	
Mary Knights	3	
Rhoda Ling	15	Gen. Servant
James Cross	45	Lodger / lab.

40: Railway Cottage:

William Edwards	42	Lab.
Harriot Edwards	42	Wife
Thomas Edwards	7	
Mary A. Edwards	4	
Charlotte E. Edwards	1	

41: Railway Cottage:

James Heowend?	30	Lab
Charlotte Heowend?	26	Wife
James Heowend?	7mths.	

Berney Arms Remembered

21: Marsh House (near 7-mile house)

James Thaxter	36	Unmarried farmer 20 acres
Maria Thaxter	67	Mother/ housekeeper
Maria Thaxter	36	Sister/unmarried/ dairymaid
Walter Thaxter	4	Nephew

22: Marsh House (Seven Mile House):

James Burgess	65	Farmer 64 acres employs 5 men
Elizabeth Burgess	58	Wife
Joseph Burgess	23	Marsh lab.
Abraham Burgess	18	Marsh lab.
Benjamin Burgess	13	Grandson
Elizabeth High	16	Dairymaid
Sarah A. Calver	12	Servant- housemaid (previously at Berney cottages)

23: Cottage (No. 1 ?)

James Calver	66	Cement Lab.
Mary Calver	61	Wife
George Burcham	28	Lodger/ Cement lab.

1 Unit to Let. (No. 2 Cottage?)

24: Cottage (No. 3?):

William Hanton	44	Ag.lab
Annie Hanton	49	Wife
Maria Hanton	20	Daughter/servant
Caroline Hanton	11	

25: Cottage (No. 4?)

John Burgess	36	Marshman (at 7-Mile House. in 1841, and at Ashtree Farm in 1871)
Harriet Burgess	31	Wife
Jane Burgess	7	
Robert Thaxter	23	Lodger / marshman (living at house by 7-mile in 1841, & at Berney Inn in 1891)
Elizabeth Thaxter	26	

26: Marsh House (Ashtree Farm?):

Horace Gilbert	45	Marsh farmer
Emily Gilbert	44	Wife
Charles Gilbert	22	Marshfarmer
Martha Gilbert	18	Dressmaker
Fredrick Gilbert	16	
Mary Gilbert	14	
Sarah Gilbert	13	
Susannah Gilbert	10	
Susannah Beck	71	Mother-in-law
George Smith	17	Lodger / Shepard

27: Private House (Bungalow?):

Robert Bull	40	Lab. Cement Works
Maria Bull	32	Wife
Charles Bull	7	
Maria Bull	4	
George Bull	2	
Mary Bacon	72	Visitor

28: Cottage (No. 6):

William Milligan	47	Mariner
Esther Milligan	46	Wife
Sarah Milligan	11	
Thomas	9	
Elizabeth	6	
Edward	2	

29: Cottage (No. 7):

Charles Eason	40	Lab. Cement Works
Elizabeth Eason	36	Wife

30: Berney Arms Inn:

James Knights	32	Innkeeper (from Runham)
Maria Knights	35	Wife (nee Green, from Winterton)
Ellis Knights	10	
George Knights	8	
Henry Knights	6	
Johnathan Knights	3	
Ann Long	16	Visitor
John Green	17	Visitor/ nephew from Rollesby
Alfred Juhhall	32	Visitor

31: Cottage (Station):

George Pert	43	Platelayer E.C. Railway
Mary Pert	52	Wife
Henry Pert	19	Platelayer E.C. Railway

32: Cottage (Station):

William Booty	32	Platelayer E.C. Railway
Mary Booty	30	Wife
Caroline Booty	1	

1851 Census: (March 30-31st) Ref HO107/1819.

3: (house near 7-mile house)

Joseph Thaxter	65	Ag. lab / marshman born at Burgh
Maria Thaxter	55	Wife
James Thaxter	26	Son / ag. Lab.) twin
Maria Thaxter	26	Marsh lab.) twin
Henry Thaxter	24	,, ,, (marshman at Ravenhall on Island in 1881)

George Thaxter	22	" " (a farmer in Halvergate in 1861)
Harriet Thaxter	20	
Robert Thaxter	13	Grandson (at Berney cottages in 1861 & at Berney
Inn in 1891)		
William Thaxter	5	,, ,,

4: Seven Mile House:

James Burgess	53	Marshman / Ag.Lab (born at Burgh Castle)
Elizabeth Burgess	49	Wife
Frederick Burgess	28	Ag. Lab
James Burgess	16	Ag. Lab.
Joseph Burgess	14	Ag. Lab
Shadrack Burgess	12	
Abraham Burgess	8	

5: (cottage no.1?):

James Calver	56	Rail Lab.
Mary Calver	50	Wife
Charles Calver	15	
Phoebe Clark	18	House servant

6: (cottage no.2?)

John Calver	27	Ag. Lab.
Maria Calver	25	Wife
Sarah Ann Calver	2	(at 7-mile house in 1861)
Sophie Calver	1	
James Calver	1 mth.	

7: (Ashtree Farm?):

James Duffield	63	Widowed / Marshfarmer 234 acres (born at Tunstall)
Henry Duffield	34	Farmers son (born Freethorpe)
Mary Wigg	42	Unmarried housekeeper
Mary Dyballs	20	Dairymaid
Elizabeth Gibbs	20	Housemaid
George ?	15	Servant

2 houses uninhabited (cottages 3 & 4?)

8: (Bungalow?):

James Duffield	44	Ag. Lab. (born Freethorpe)
Mary Ann Duffield	43	Wife (born Burgh Castle)
James Duffield	5	
Frances Duffield	1	
Daniel Duffield	3	

9: (cottage no 6?):

Joshua Clark	27	Ag.Lab
Sarah Clark	23	Wife (middle name Anne nee Burrage)
Emily Allen	24	Visitor (nee Burrage)
Margaret Burrage	56	Nurse (mother to Sarah & Emily above)

Margaret Clark	1 mth.	
10: (cottage No. 7?):		
Abraham Gowen	27	Carpenter (born at Raven Hall on Island)
Jane Gowen	30	Wife
11: (Berney Inn):		
Horace Gilbert	35	Innkeeper
Emily Gilbert	35	Wife
Charles Gilbert	12	
Martha Gilbert	6	
Fred Gilbert	5	
Mary Ann Gilbert	4	
Sarah A. Gilbert	3	
Mary Beck	25	Unmarried dressmaker/ visitor
Eleanor Beck	21	Unmarried
unnamed Gilbert	1mth	Daughter
12: (station cottage?):		
Thomas Pickering	29	Rail Lab.
Sarah Pickering	25	Wife
James Pickering	1	
13: (station cottage?):		
George Warner	34	Rail Lab.
Emily Warner	29	Wife/ dressmaker
Amelia Warner	7	
Anne A. Warner	3	
Georgiana Warner	2	

1841 Census (15th June) (785/12)

It is not possible to be sure which entries are at Berney Arms but the following are likely, some having been deduced from the Tithe Apportionment.

This entry is probably for the marsh house next to Polkeys Mill:

Joseph Thaxter	45	Marshman
Maria Thaxter	40	
Robert Thaxter	19	
James Thaxter	17	
Maria Thaxter	17	
Henry Thaxter	14	
George Thaxter	11	
Harriet Thaxter	8	
Robert Thaxter	4	(living at Berney cottages in 1861 as marshman)

The next listed entry is: (so is this another building here next to Polkey's?)

Joseph Thaxter	20	Marshman (probably the son of the above Joseph!)
Ann Thaxter	20	

Berney Arms Remembered

This entry is probably for 7-Mile House.

James Burgess	40	Marshfarmer
Elizabeth Burgess	35	
John Burgess	17	(later at cottages in 1861 & Ashtree Farm in 1871 as marshman)
George Burgess	15	(later marshman in 1861 at Wickhampton)
Fred Burgess	9	
James Burgess	5	
Joseph Burgess	3	
Shadrack Burgess	1	
Susan Eliz Burgess	13	

This is probably Ashtree farmhouse:

James Duffield	50	Farmer
Caroline Duffield	20	
James Duffield	30	
Henry Duffield	25	
Francis Duffield	24	
George Duffield	20	
Mary Porter	20	Servant
Ann Mingay	19	Servant
Fred Mingay	20	servant

This may be the Berney Arms Inn.

Robert Rushmer	30	Innkeeper
Mary Rushmer	30	

****

RAILWAY COTTAGES NEAR 7-MILE – WICKHAMPTON CENSUS

1901 (RG13/1855)

Entry No. 121 – By Railway

Robert Smith	31	Platelayer
Eliza Smith	32	Wife
Sidney Edwards	14	Stepson
Harriet Edwards	12	Stepdaughter
Maud Edwards	10	Stepdaughter
William Edwards	72	Platelayer

Entry No. 122 – By Railway

Edward Pettingill	35	Railway navvy

| Charlotte Pettingill | 30 | Wife |
| Thomas Pettingill | 5 | |

Entry No. 123 – By Railway

| Eleanor Lubbock | 58 | Wife |
| John Lubbock | 26 | Son Railway navvy |

1891 (RG1539)
Entry No. 162

John Andrew	27	Platelayer
Sarah Andrew	26	
Robert Andrew	11	
William Andrew	9	
Arthur Andrew	7	
Frederick Andrew	5	
Ethel Andrew	3	
Lucy Andrew	1	

No. 163

William Lubbock	55	Platelayer
Eleanor Lubbock	42	
Clara Lubbock	25	
John Lubbock	15	
Eleanor Lubbock	14	
Edith Lubbock	7	
Florence Lubbock	6	
Alice Lubbock	3	

No. 164

John Burgess	65	Marshman
Harriet Burgess	67	
Ernest Hubbard	16	Farm Lab.

1881 (RG1961)
No. 192

| William Halesworth | 47 | Marshman |
| Susanna Halesworth | 50 | |

No. 193

William Lubbock	47	Platelayer
Eleanor Lubbock	39	
Clara Lubbock	15	
Ann Lubbock	10	
Betsy Lubbock	8	
John Lubbock	6	
Eleanor Lubbock	4	

Harriet Lubbock	2	

No. 194

Henry Rushmer	47	Platelayer
Harriet Rushmer	47	
William Rushmer	22	Platelayer
George Rushmer	18	Platelayer
Rosanna Rushmer	14	
Thomas Rushmer	13	
Marilyn Rushmer	9	
Arthur Rushmer	6	
Ernest Rushmer	2	
Lily Rushmer	1mth.	

1871 (RG1829)
No. 1 On the railway

William Halesworth	37	Lab (probably a marsh lab)
Susanna Halesworth	40	

No. 2

William Lubbock	39	Railway Lab
Eleanor Lubbock	29	
Mary Lubbock	10	
Clarisa Lubbock	6	
Elizabeth Lubbock	4	
Ann Lubbock	10mth	

No. 3

Henry Rushmer	37	Platelayer
Harriet Rushmer	37	
William Rushmer	12	
George Rushmer	8	
Alice Rushmer	6	
Rosanna Rushmer	4	
Thomas Rushmer	3	
Joseph Rushmer	1	

1861 (RG1227)
No. 1 Railway House

William Halesworth	20	Marshman
Susanna Halesworth	30	

No. 2 Railway House

George Shearing	20	Platelayer
Louise Shearing	30	

No. 3 Railway House

Joseph Dunson	30	Platelayer from South Repps

Hapzibetly Duncan	34	Wife from Somerleyton
Hannah Duncan	10	
Maria Duncan	9	
Jane Duncan	6	
Charles Duncan	4	
Ellenor Duncan	2	
Elizabeth Duncan	1	

1851 (HO1819)
No. 1

Thomas Kettle	35	Railway lab
Elizabeth Kettle	42	
Eliza Kettle	7	
John Burgess	24	Lodger / marsh lab.

No. 2

John Brinded	36	Railway lab.
Eleanor Brinded	32	
Elizabeth Graves	66	Widow

No. 3

William Boast	33	Railway lab.
Louisa Boast	30	

1841 (785/12)
No Railway houses existed at this time.

****

LOCKGATE FARM AND LOCKGATE MILL – FREETHORPE CENSUSES
These entries are for the Lockgate Mill marsh house and Lockgate Farm in the Detached Freethorpe Parish. It is not possible to tell from the censuses which is the farm and which is the mill marsh house.

1901 (RG13/1855)
No. 97 Lockgate Level of Marshes Detached Portion of Parish

Daniel Banham	48	Marsh farmer
Jane Banham	48	Wife
William Banham	18	Ag. lab/ farm worker
Christiana Banham	22	Dom serv
Charles King	25	Boarder/ ag lab
George Watling	25	,, ,,
? Jones?	14	Nephew from Halvergate/ bricklayer/labourer

No. 98 Lockgate Level of Marshes Detached Portion of Parish

James Banham	39	Marshman (son of James & Ann Maria Banham who were at Upper Seven Mile House on the Detached Chedgrave Marshes on The Island)
Sarah Banham	36	Wife
Lucy Banham	14	
Benjamin Banham	7	
William Banham	2	
Robert Banham	26	Single – nephew / marshman
Edward Aldis	17	Single – lodger / railway navvy
Anna Aldis	21	Single – general servant
Violet Head	15	Lodger – general servant

1891
No. 96

Daniel Banham	38	Marshman (son of Last Banham, full name Daniel Key Banham)
Jane Banham	38	Wife (nee Smith?)
Margaret Banham	18	
Mary A. Banham	16	
Christiana Banham	12	
George Smith	15	Marshman / lodger

No. 97

John Smith	63	Marshman
Eliza Smith	63	
Fred Smith	21	Marshman
Susana Smith	18	
Charles Garwood	5	Nephew
Edward Hanton	17	Lodger / railway lab.

1881 (RG11/1961)
No. 1 marsh house

Daniel Key Banham	28	Marshman (a son of Last Banham)
Jane Anna Banham	28	(nee Smith?)
Betsy Banham	8	
Susan Mary Ann Banham	6	
Sarah Ann Banham	4	
Christiana Jane Banham	2	
Un-named Banham	5days	
Jane Banham	17	
Margaret Jones	20	Sister
Herbert Jones	1mth	

Berney Arms Remembered

No. 2

James Key	73	
Sarah Key	69	
Alice Walters?	12	Granddaughter

1871 (RG10/1829)
No. 101

Henry Thaxter	35(?)	Occupation not given! (Probably a marshman He was at the marsh house near 7-mile House in 1841 & 1851 and was marshman at Ravenhall on the Island in 1881 & 1891)
Mary Thaxter	40	
Charlotte Thaxter	9	

No. 99 (Probably Lockgate Farm)

George Smith	51	Marsh farmer
Mary Ann Smith	40	
Fred Smith	19	Millwright
Mary Ann Smith	11	
Daniel? Smith	4	
William Smith	3	
Jane Thaxter	16	Servant
William Pigmy	40	Dom serv
Sam Clark	30	Lodger / lab
Elizabeth Clark	27	

No. 98

| Charles Forder | 45 | Thatcher |
| Rebecca Forder | 42 | |

1861 (RG9/1227)
No. 1 (Probably Lockgate Farm)

George Smith	41	Marsh farmer
Mary Ann Smith	31	
Fred Smith	12	
Mary Ann Smith	6	
Sarah A. Browne	21	Dairymaid
Tabitha Banham	18	Housemaid (maybe daughter of Ben & Kirun Banham then at Ashtree farm, Acle New Rd.)

No. 2

James Key	53	Ag. Lab
Sarah Key	52	
Daniel Key	20	
Mary Ann Key	18	
Edward Key	16	

148

Emily Key	12
Jane Key	9

1851 (HO107/1819)

Only one marshman listed:

No. 22 (Probably Lockgate Farm)

George Smith	30	Marshman / Ag. Lab.
Mary Ann Smith	22	
Fred Clark	2	

1841 (753)

Only one marshman listed: (Probably Lockgate Farm)

John Withers	35	Marshman
Mary Withers	35	Wife
George Smith	15	
Martha Tary(?)	20	

BIBLIOGRAPHY & REFERENCES:

Martin George, The Land Use, Ecology and Conservation of Broadland, 1992, ISBN 185341 0470.
Tom Williamson, The Norfolk Broads: A Landscape Survey, 1997. ISBN 071904801x
Martin Ewans, The Battle for the Broads, 1992, ISBN 0861380924.
Sheila Hutchinson, Berney Arms: Past & Present, 2000.
Sheila Hutchinson, The Halvergate Fleet: Past & Present, 2001, ISBN 0954168305.
Sheila Hutchinson, The Island (The Haddiscoe Island): Past & Present, 2002, ISBN 0954168313
A.J. Ward, unpublished notes, held by the Norfolk Windmills Trust.
A.J. Ward, 'Smoke Drifting Over the Reeds' in Journal of the Norfolk Industrial Archaeology Society, Vol 6, No 4, 1999 & No 5, 2000
Arthur C. Smith, Drainage Windmills of the Norfolk Marshes, 1990.
Robert Malster, Wherries and Waterways, 1986.
Robert Malster, The Broads, 1993. ISBN 0850338603.
Roy Clark, Black Sailed Traders, 1961, ISBN 0715354434
A.H. Patterson, Wildlife on a Norfolk Estuary, 1907.
Census Records 1841,1851,1861,1871,1881,1891,1901 held at Norfolk Records Office.
Kelly's Handbooks of Titled, Landed & Official Classes, 1889, 1925, 1937, 1962.
Kelly's Directories for Norfolk, 1892, 1900, 1904, 1908, 1912, 1916,1937.
White's Directories, 1836, 1845, 1854, 1864, 1883.
Harrod's Norfolk Directory, 1868.

SOME USEFUL WEBSITES:

http://www.berneyarms.co.uk
http://www.hutchson.freeserve.co.uk/STARTHERE
http://www.old-maps.co.uk
http://www.wherrylines.org.uk
http://www.accessgenealogy.com
http://www.familysearch.org
http://www.windmillworld.com
http://www.uea.ac.uk

The author on the river wall in 1999.
Polkey's mill and Seven-Mile House are to the left
and Cadge's mill is to the right in the distance.

Other books by the Author.
Berney Arms: Past & Present. Pub. 2000
The Halvergate Fleet: Past & Present. ISBN 0 9541683 0 5 Pub. 2001
The Island (The Haddiscoe Island):Past & Present. ISBN 0 9541683 1 3 Pub 2002